Object Lessons with Paper and Scissors

By

HAROLD P. WELLS

MOODY PRESS

CHICAGO

Contents

Introduction

Audiovisuals appeal to children and adults alike. Especially is this true when they contain the element of mystery or surprise. Thus, in the hands of a Christian worker, paper and scissors can become two very important tools for conveying the wonderful truths of the Word of God to children.

A problem arising when anyone proposes a new or varied teaching method is that some teachers may be unwilling to consider its merits. They are afraid, for one reason or another, to launch out and give the suggestion an honest try. Perhaps one reason for this attitude is that many individuals who accept positions of leadership in the field of religious education are content with the traditional methods and therefore see no need for innovative ideas.

On the other hand, I am sure there are those who just lack the self-confidence necessary to step out and experiment. They feel they are not sufficiently trained or endowed with the ability to use a new teaching medium that appears to be complicated.

So before you read any further, let me put you at ease by stating that I am convinced that anyone who really loves teaching and children can learn to skillfully and effectively use paper folding and cutting to present the spiritual truths of the Bible to boys and girls. Numerous ministers, Sunday school teachers, missionaries, and other religious workers around the world, because of their desire to become better teachers and by simply following instructions, have found this art medium to be one of the most effective and fascinating methods of teaching they have ever used. I feel confident that you also will find that the effort and time spent in preparing to use this method of illustrating biblical truths are well worthwhile.

The familiar saying "In one ear and out the other" is often true. However, have you ever heard anyone make the statement "In one eye and out the other"? No, for it is a proved fact that the mind retains a greater percentage of that which is seen and heard at the same time than of that which is merely heard. Visually illustrated scriptural lessons therefore can be tremendously effective because a child (or adult) is less likely to forget what he sees, especially when the element of the unexpected is present.

We must also take into consideration the fact that the present generation of children is highly visually oriented due to television and the methods of teaching in school. Thus, the average child today is quickly turned off by any teaching method that is basically verbal in nature. In order to attract and keep his interest, we must use varied types of visual media. So paper folding and cutting can become a valuable hook upon which the student can mentally hang the spiritual truths a teacher is endeavoring to convey. Through this medium, the message presented enters both the eye and the ear, making it extremely effective as a teaching tool.

The use of visual aids as a teaching medium is by no means a twentieth-century marvel. God was the first to use this dynamic method of teaching. After the Flood, He set a rainbow in the sky as a visual confirmation of His covenant with mankind never to destroy the world in this manner again (Gen. 9).

Another visual object lesson of the Old Testament was the memorial built by the people of Israel after they had crossed the Jordan River. God instructed that a man from each tribe was to take a stone from the river and place it where the tribes lodged. Their leader, Joshua, said, "This [will] be a sign among you, that when your children ask their fathers in time to come, saying, What mean ye by these stones? Then ye shall answer them, That the waters of Jordan were cut off before the ark of the covenant of the LORD; when it passed over Jordan . . . and these stones shall be for a memorial unto the children of Israel for ever" (Josh. 4:6-7).

God often directed the Old Testament prophets to perform symbolic acts that were nothing more than effective, perceptual object lessons through which they presented to God's people His message. By the use of this technique, the people of Israel more easily understood the spiritual truths God wished to convey to them through His prophets.

A thorough examination of the gospels will reveal how Jesus Christ also used this graphic style of teaching. In fact, the church today still uses two God-ordained object lessons through which the gospel is proclaimed: baptism and the Lord's Supper. Thus, one can readily see that both the Old and New Testaments made use of visual sermons as the media through which God's message was presented.

If the use of object lessons was considered to be an important method of teaching spiritual truths in biblical times, how much more significant should be its use in the twentieth century where the majority of people have become visually oriented. There is no doubt in my mind that the use of object lessons can greatly assist you in making the teaching-learning process more challenging, interesting, and permanent. This is true of all types of audio-visual aids, including the art of paper folding and cutting. Variety is important in effective teaching. Thus, you should be selective and use the most graphic and dynamic visual aids available to you.

However, if any aid is to be effective, the art medium used must only be a means to an end, not an end in itself. A visual aid is to create interest and to illustrate visually the spiritual truth you are seeking to impart. It is merely a window to allow the light of God's truth to enter the minds of your pupils. Never lose sight of the fact that the message must at all times be uppermost in your presentation. You will have been a failure if all your audience can remember, after you have completed your sermon or talk, is your skill in paper folding or the effect produced by that skill. However, you will have been a success if the effect is remembered as a mental hook upon which your students have hung the spiritual truth you were endeavoring to convey.

Be careful not to fall into the old trap of thinking that a visual aid is a means of helping the teacher get by with little or no preparation, or that it is a fine time filler. To be skillful in the use of visual aids, especially in the art of paper folding and cutting, a substantial amount of preparation is necessary. Each object lesson must be mastered, if it is to be done effectively and convincingly. You cannot afford to look clumsy or give the appearance of being an amateur. Learning to be a professional at paper folding and cutting requires much practice, time, and patience. There is no shortcut to success in this field.

Again, take care that you do not use this art media solely for the sake of entertainment. Its primary purpose is to add to the effectiveness of the message, not to distract from it. You are not in front of your audience to display your wonderful talent. You are before it as a servant of God to present an important message from God's eternal Word.

In the pages that follow, you will find tested object lessons that use the art medium of paper folding and cutting. You may not wish to use the message material exactly as suggested, but, through studying the material, you may be stimulated to create messages of your own for use with the effects.

Adapt each object lesson and message to your own personality style. The main purpose of this book is to stimulate your thinking. There is no doubt in my mind that the time and energy you spend in developing your technique in paper folding and cutting will be personally rewarding and will greatly increase your ability to effectively touch lives with the gospel. To this end these object lessons are shared with you. Read through them carefully, think creatively, and rich blessings await you through the use of this simple art form.

Guidelines for Using Paper and Scissors to Illustrate the Word of God

From my personal experience in presenting messages, devotionals, or biblical lessons using paper folding and cutting, I would like to submit some basic guidelines that may be helpful to you.

1. *Never* attempt even the most simple paper folding and cutting effect until you have spent sufficient time practicing and feel reasonably comfortable in your ability to do it well.

2. *Always* remember that you are before your audience to present a spiritual lesson. Therefore, you should spend an adequate amount of time in meditation and prayer before each presentation. The leadership of the Holy Spirit in your life is imperative if the truths of God's Word are to penetrate the hearts and minds of your listeners. You are but an instrument through whom the Holy Spirit does His work. He, and He alone, brings about conviction of sin and guides individuals into an understanding of all truth (John 16: 5-11).

3. *Rehearse your message,* not only to be sure of its content, but to be sure you know where in the message you plan to fold and cut the paper. This is essential! If you have children at home, practice your object

lesson before them. They will enjoy it, and also you will be able to see how the overall presentation is received and understood. Ask for feedback. See if they know the theme of the message and fully understand the basic spiritual truths presented. This will help you to know whether or not your message is simple enough to be easily understood by your audience.

4. When presenting object lessons, *do not talk down* to your audience. Beware of using a soft, pious-sounding, or fairy-tale-type voice. Be natural.

5. *Never* give the impression that you think that you are superior to your audience or that you possess any unique talent. Your purpose is to teach an important scriptural lesson. Guard against a look-what-I-can-do facial or bodily expression or attitude.

6. *Remember*, you are not a performer. You are not there for the purpose of putting on an entertainment program per se. You are an ambassador, a representative of Jesus Christ. Therefore, at all times endeavor to maintain an atmosphere of dignity and reverence. If you do not, the overall effectiveness of your presentation will be greatly diminished.

7. *Learn* in advance as much as you can about the audience to which you will be speaking. The more you know about the listeners, the easier it will be for you to decide how best to adapt your presentation to meet their spiritual needs and the intellectual level of the majority present. Be flexible, either simplifying or adding more details, depending upon your audience and the occasion.

8. *Never rush* through the paper folding and cutting. On the other hand, do not make the mistake of drawing it out too long. Practice and learn to coordinate each

part of the effect with your message so that each complements the other. This will add greatly to the impact of your conclusion. Make sure that enough time is spent showing clearly what you have cut, and that everyone fully understands its relationship to the truth you are emphasizing.

Unless your audience is fully aware of what is taking place, the cogency of your message will be lost. Your task is to make sure the truth you wish to convey is understood. The result is the work of the Holy Spirit.

9. *If you must use theological terms* in your message, be sure that you fully explain what they mean in simple, everyday language. Never take for granted that your audience knows the meaning of *redemption, atonement, born again, grace, incarnation,* and so on. Avoid if at all possible the use of long, technical, or theological words. This is especially true when talking to children, but it is also applicable when speaking to the average adult audience.

10. *Make sure* that the paper you use for each of your effects is large enough to be seen by everyone in the audience. If a particular effect requires the use of a small piece of paper, as some will, then use it with small groups only.

If at all possible, utilize a well-lighted platform for your presentation. This will help everyone see what is going on during the message and will make the object lesson more meaningful.

11. *Always radiate* an atmosphere of enjoyment and enthusiasm. In working with children, your personality will speak more loudly than your words. Let them know through your facial expressions, tone of voice, and body language that what you have to say is tre-

mendously important. Let them sense by your actions and expression that you are truly happy to have the opportunity of sharing the good news of Jesus Christ with them. Never give the impression through non-verbal communication that you are bored or that your subject is not of great importance to you.

12. *Prior planning* is essential. See that everything you need is ready ahead of time. Always have extra sheets of paper ready. There will be those times when you will make a mistake, so be prepared. Make sure the scissors are sharp and in good working condition. Never take anything for granted. Check and double-check; this will avoid embarrassment and will help give you the needed self-confidence to expend your energy on the most important thing—your message.

13. *Do not allow a mistake* or any other distraction to disturb you. If you should make a wrong fold or cut, just put aside the piece of paper, take another sheet, and start again. Always remember to act natural.

14. This art medium can be used in a *number of ways.* Its only limitations are your own imagination and creativity. Some ways in which I have used it most effectively are:

    a. by combining two or more of the paper folding and cutting effects into a full sermon, using them as illustrative material

    b. as the main thrust of a talk for youth, women's or men's groups

    c. as an introduction to, or illustration of, the Sunday school lesson

    d. as a devotional at any group meeting, such as, vacation Bible school, Christian day camp, backyard summer fun program, or retreat

e. as part of the worship service to illustrate the theme of a hymn

f. as a means of launching a discussion on some biblical subject at the midweek prayer service or home Bible study group

g. as the children's sermon at the Sunday worship service or during evangelistic meetings.

15. *Remember* that all children like to participate in physical activities. They are also interested in trying something that is challenging and new. Give each child a pair of scissors and a sheet of paper. As you tell the story, let the children follow as you fold and cut your larger piece of paper. Do it slowly so they can easily follow each step in the folding and cutting process. They will be surprised at their ability to do the same thing and produce the same effect as you.

A word of caution—when using this method of teaching, be sure the effect you choose is one simple enough to be accomplished by all the children in the group.

Make sure your instructions are clearly given so that each child can succeed. Do not allow anyone to become embarrassed by failure to achieve the desired results. If done correctly, the folding and cutting activity will enhance the learning process.

16. Finally, if you do not really enjoy using object lessons, or do not have a love for children, *do not* use this medium of visual education. Anticipate some interruptions; do not allow yourself to be disturbed by them. Exhibit at all times a truly Christian spirit of understanding and caring.

1

Truehearted Soldiers

(Judg. 6-7)

Materials Needed:

A sheet of white paper or newspaper, approximately
8½"×11½"

A pair of scissors

A fine-point black felt pen or black press-on lettering

Instructions for Paper Fold and Cut:

Draw on the sheet of paper a large heart (fig. 1.1). Then print on the heart the wording shown in figure 1.1.

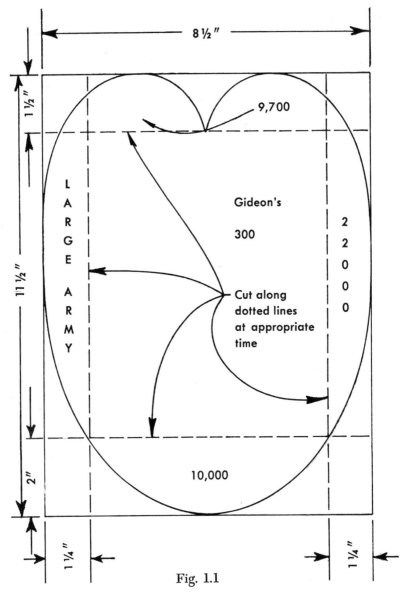

Fig. 1.1

18

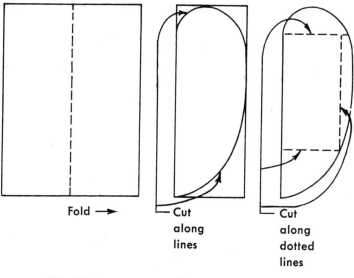

Fold →

Cut along lines

Cut along dotted lines

Fig. 1.2   Fig. 1.3   Fig. 1.4

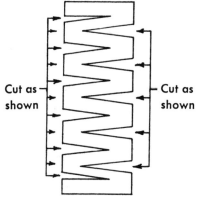

Cut as shown   Cut as shown

Fig. 1.5

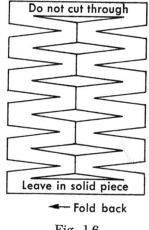

Do not cut through

Leave in solid piece

← Fold back

Fig. 1.6

19

Open out for step-through opening

Fig. 1.7

First, fold the sheet of paper in half as in figures 1.2 and 1.3. Trim off the edges of the paper, forming the shape of a heart (see figs. 1.3 and 1.4).

Second, show the heart to the audience. Say you plan to cut a hole in it big enough for a child to step through. Cut off the top, side, and bottom of the heart, after it has been refolded as shown in figure 1.4. Or this may be done as you relate the story of Gideon as recorded in Judges 6 and 7 (see fig. 1.1). This is the method I use, and it is far more effective.

Third, fold the sheet of paper in half again and cut along the alternate lines, being careful not to cut all the way through (see fig. 1.5). Be sure you cut the center line *only* from the bottom to the top cuts in the paper. It is important that you leave the top and bottom sections of the sheet of paper solid, and the middle cuts should only be approxi-

20

mately three-fourths of the way through. This is shown in figures 1.5 and 1.6.

Fourth, reopen the sheet of paper. It should now look like figure 1.7. When open to its fullest extent, the hole should be large enough for a child to step easily through it. This may appear impossible, but it can be done. However, be careful in opening the sheet of paper. It will be very fragile at the edges and can easily be torn.

Message:

Read carefully Judges 6-7, especially noting chapter 7. As you begin to relate the story of Gideon's call from God to save the people of Israel from the Midianites, show your audience the sheet of paper with the heart drawn on it.

Tell how God told Gideon that he had far too many soldiers for the task He wanted him to perform. God wanted Israel to be convinced that it was not by their might that they were victorious over Midian. He wanted them to know their victory over the enemy was through the miraculous power of the God of their father Abraham. God did not want Israel to proudly say, "Mine own hand hath saved me" (Judg. 7:2). (*At this point, fold the paper in half and cut out the shape of the heart by trimming off the edges of the paper [see figs. 1.2 and 1.3]. Then show the heart to your audience.*)

Gideon did what any good commander would do. He decided first to get rid of those in his ranks who were fearful of going into battle. So he told those who were afraid to go back home. (*Cut off the edges of the heart that have printed on them "Large Army" and "22,000" [see fig. 1.1]*).

God informed Gideon that his army was still too large. He instructed Gideon to test the remaining ten thousand men to find out who were the really truehearted soldiers (Judges 7:4-8).

Following Gideon's test, only 300 soldiers were left to go into battle. (*At this point, cut off the top and bottom edges of the heart, which are marked "10,000" and "9,700" [see fig. 1.1]*).

Relate the amazing story of how Gideon, with only 300 soldiers left, was victorious by the power of God. Conclude by stating that this seemingly impossible feat was accomplished because Gideon's faith was in God. Ask your listeners if they would have believed it possible for Gideon and only 300 men to have conquered the armies of the Midianites and Amalekites. This was a seemingly impossible feat, but through faith it was accomplished.

Announce that you will illustrate the teaching of this story by using the remainder of the sheet of paper. Remind the audience that almost half the sheet has been cut away, yet you will cut a hole in it large enough to allow a person to step all the way through. You may wish to emphasize that perhaps many present do not believe this feat is possible. Their lack of faith is reasonable when you compare the size of the paper with the size of the person who is to step through it. What they need to do is exercise faith in you that you will somehow be able to bring it to pass. So ask them to watch very carefully.

Now fold the sheet of paper in half and follow the instructions as given in Instructions for Paper Fold and Cut, steps three and four. Study carefully figures 1.5, 1.6, and 1.7. Be sure you cut the center line *only* from the bottom to the top cuts in the paper. Do not cut all the way through (see fig. 1.6). The results will be a circular border large enough for a person to step through easily (see fig. 1.7).

Conclude your message by saying something to this effect: "You have just seen demonstrated what appeared to be an impossible feat. You saw a person actually step through a sheet of paper much smaller in size than he/she was. I was able to accomplish this seemingly impossible feat because I knew the correct way to fold and cut the paper. God can do many things that to us may appear impossible, because He knows the 'how' by which to bring things to pass. So God, with whom all things are possible through faith, was able to use Gideon and his 300 truehearted soldiers to win a great battle and bring victory to the people of Israel.

"So never say that something just cannot be done. Have faith, and you will be surprised how many things that appear to be impossible can be accomplished by the power and wisdom of God, provided our faith is grounded in Jesus Christ, His Son, and our Savior."

NOTE: You will find this effect has many applications. However, it should never be used the second time before the same audience. Should you do so, you will find that it loses its impact. It is also important that you practice a few times in private before using this effect before an audience. Be sure that you know the procedure well enough so that you do not have to concentrate on the folding and cutting. Rather your concentration can be focused on the telling of the story.

You may, depending on the occasion and time, wish to continue your message by talking about how important it is today that God have courageous, truehearted soldiers to do His work. Much that needs to be accomplished may at first appear impossible, but with God on our side we will be amazed at what can be done.

Other passages of Scripture you may wish to refer to are: Zechariah 4:6; Matthew 19:26; Mark 9:23; 10:27; 14:36a; Romans 8:14-17, 28-39; 1 Corinthians 4:2; Ephesians 3:16-21; 6:10-18; Philippians 4:13; and Revelation 17:14.

2

Made Whole Through Forgiveness

(Gen. 37–47)

Materials Needed:

Three pieces of crepe paper, approximately 3′×2″
A pair of sharp scissors

Instructions for Paper Fold and Cut:

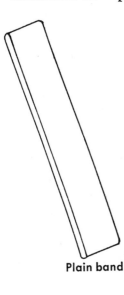

Plain band

Band with two
twists

Band with one
twist

Fig. 2.1

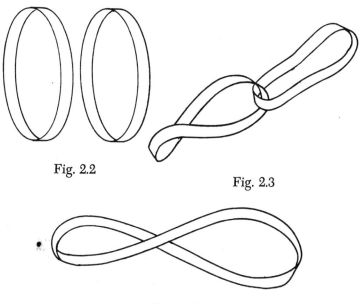

Fig. 2.2

Fig. 2.3

Fig. 2.4

Prepare three pieces of crepe paper as in figure 2.1. Glue one band at the ends to form a plain single band. Form the second band by making a full turn in the crepe paper before gluing the ends. Prepare the third by making a half turn in the crepe paper before gluing the ends.

First, take the plain band and cut it down the middle and separate it into two bands (see fig. 2.2). To cut the band, insert the scissor point into the center of the band and begin to cut it in half. All three bands must be cut in the same manner or the effect will be given away and lose its impact.

Second, take the band with the complete turn in the crepe paper and cut it down the center in the same manner as you did the plain band. Now, instead of two separate bands, you have two bands linked together as in figure 2.3.

Third, take the band with the half turn in the crepe paper and cut it down the center in the same manner as you did with bands one and two. Now you will have one large band, twice the size of the one you began with (see fig. 2.4).

Message:

Begin by telling the story of Joseph and his brothers as recorded in Genesis 37. Give as many details as you wish and/or time permits. However, the major emphasis should be on the jealousy and hatred of the brothers toward Joseph because of their father's love for him (Gen. 37:3-4).

This deep-rooted ill will separated Joseph and his brothers and resulted in the brothers' plot to get rid of him. Ultimately Joseph was sold into slavery to the Egyptians. (*Demonstrate this separation by cutting the plain band and showing how the band has become two separate ones.*)

Joseph felt love and concern for his brothers in spite of what they had done to him. He still longed to be near them. He never forgot them. Tell of Joseph's experiences while in Egypt, and how God used the evil designs of his brothers to accomplish His will. Mention the great famine, which eventually drove Joseph's brothers to Egypt to purchase grain. Use as many details from chapters 42 and 43 as you feel necessary. Emphasize that Joseph recognized his brothers even though they did not recognize him.

(*Following this part of your message, take the band with the full turn in it and cut it down the center. The single band will now become two bands linked together. This will demonstrate the point that though separated physically from his family because of his brothers' jealousy and hatred, Joseph was still linked to them by love.*)

Tell of Joseph's forgiveness of his brothers and their reconciliation. (*Take the band with the half turn in it and cut it down the center. It will become one large band, twice the size of the original one. This will graphically illustrate the point that, through love and forgiveness, the family of Joseph was brought back together and made one again.*) You may wish to conclude your message at this point.

However, this experience from the life of Joseph offers an opportunity of drawing a parallel between this story and that of the Fall of man. Tell of God's continued love for man in spite of his rebellious spirit and of His great desire to reconcile sinful people to Himself. He sent His only Son, Jesus Christ, into this world to die on Calvary to provide a way whereby mankind could be brought back into fellowship with God. Sinful though people are, they can be restored through faith in Jesus Christ and His atoning work. Here relate the beautiful story of reconciliation (study Eph. 2 and Col. 1-2. Other passages you may wish to refer to are John 3:16; 5:24; Rom. 3:24; 5:1-11; 2 Cor. 5:14-21; Gal. 2:16-20; 3:24-29; and Eph. 2:5, 8, 14-18).

3

Cross-bearing

(*Matt. 16:24*)

Materials Needed:

One sheet of white paper, minimum size should be 6″×
11″

One pair of sharp scissors

One black felt pen or black press-on lettering

Instructions for Paper Fold and Cut:

On a sheet of paper approximately 6″×11″, use a felt
pen to draw a line about 9 inches long that is 2¼ inches
from the right edge of the paper (see fig. 3.1). Print the
word *SIN* in large letters, in the space between the line
and the edge of the paper as in figure 3.1.

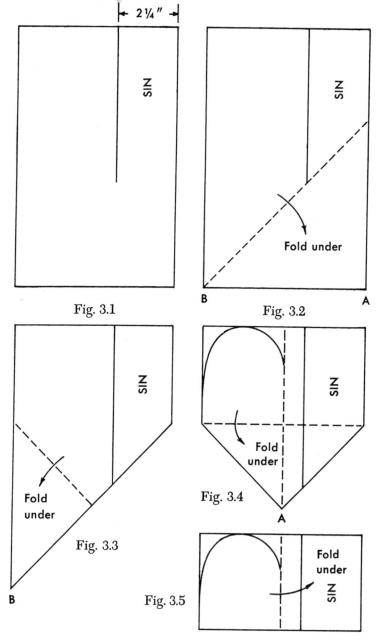

2¼"

SIN

Fig. 3.1

SIN

Fold under

B · · · · · A

Fig. 3.2

SIN

Fold under

Fig. 3.3

B

SIN

Fold under

Fig. 3.4

A

Fold under

SIN

Fig. 3.5

29

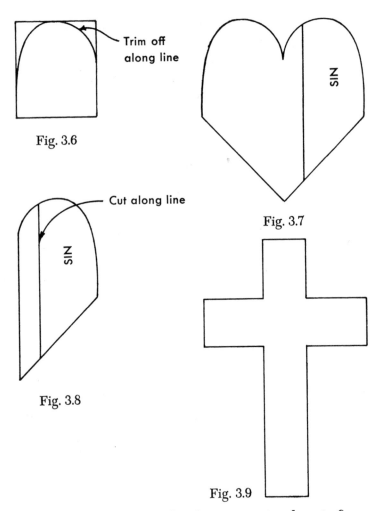

Trim off along line

Fig. 3.6

NIS

Fig. 3.7

Cut along line

NIS

Fig. 3.8

Fig. 3.9

First, fold corner A under, forming a triangle as in figure 3.2.

Second, fold corner B under in the same manner as in figure 3.3.

Third, fold the sheet in half vertically, then open it and

30

draw a rounded line to form the top of the heart as in figure 3.4.

Fourth, now fold the triangle (point A, fig. 3.4) under the top half, causing it to look like figure 3.5.

Fifth, fold the sheet of paper in half to form a square as in figure 3.6.

Sixth, cut along the line you drew to form the top of the heart (see fig. 3.6).

Seventh, open up the square but keep the two bottom folds, which form the triangle, in place. The paper will then have the shape of a heart as in figure 3.7.

Eighth, at the proper time in your message, refold the paper as in figure 3.8 and cut along the black line to remove the section marked *SIN*.

Ninth, open up the fold to form a cross as in figure 3.9. Snip off the rounded edges at the base of the cross.

Message:

Begin with the story of Adam and Eve in the Garden of Eden, as recorded in Genesis 3. Explain how sin came into the world through Adam's and Eve's disobedience, and how, since then, all mankind has been alienated from God by sin (Rom. 3:23). You might also want to refer to other passages of Scripture such as Romans 5:12-20; 6:23; and 1 John 1:8. Drive home the truth that all of us have sinned, and therefore we all fall under the condemnation of Almighty God. (*As you give the details of mankind's fall into SIN, fold the paper [see figs. 3.1-5] and trim off the top edge as in fig. 3.6. Open the paper and show your audience how it now forms the shape of a heart with the word "SIN" written on it, as in fig. 3.7.*)

Hold up the heart as you continue to talk about sin and its consequences in our lives. Be sure to explain how it is impossible for us to be able to do anything to free ourselves from the consequences of sin.

Tell the good news of God's love—that He desired to have us reconciled to Himself and therefore provided a way whereby we could be forgiven of our sins and brought back into fellowship with Him. God sent His only Son, Jesus Christ, into the world to die in order to redeem us from sin. He died in our stead and paid the total price for our redemption (John 3:16). Through the atoning work of Christ at Calvary, we can, by placing our trust in Him, be declared righteous in the sight of God (Rom. 5:9-11; 2 Cor. 5:21; Col. 1:14). (*Refold the paper [fig. 3.8] and cut along the straight line, thus cutting the word "SIN" out of the heart. Open the folded paper and reveal the cross [fig. 3.9]. You may wish to quote Rev. 1:5.*)

Conclude by telling your audience that all believers are responsible to be true disciples and cross-bearers. Since we are not saved through our good works or because of any merits of our own, but only by the love and grace of God, we should, out of thanksgiving and love, willingly, freely, and completely give ourselves in service to Christ as Master and Lord. To do this, we should deny ourselves, take up our cross, and bear it for Him (discuss Matt. 16:24-26). We are to become ambassadors (2 Cor. 5:20), witnesses (Matt 28:19-20), and proclaimers of the good news of salvation through faith in Jesus Christ.

As time permits, point out that each of us has talents that can be utilized by Christ and His church. This is our responsibility as members of Christ's Body.

Other Scripture references that can be used to develop your message are: Acts 18:27; Romans 3:24; 4:2-5; 5:20; Galatians 5:16; Ephesians 1:3-10; 2:5-10; Philippians 2:12; 1 Thessalonians 1:3-6; and Titus 3:7.

4

Witnesses for Christ

(Dan. 12:3)

Materials Needed:

Five 6-inch-square pieces of paper

One piece of thin cardboard cut in a circle approximately 3½ inches in diameter and the same color as the five squares

Five paper clips

One pair of sharp scissors

Instructions for Paper Fold and Cut:

Fold the five pieces of paper you will cut to make the individual stars as follows:

First, fold in half one 6-inch square piece of paper as in figure 4.1.

Second, fold the sheet of paper again from right to left as in figures 4.2 and 4.3. Be sure that the top of the fold is 2 inches from the top right-hand edge and the bottom of the fold is at the center of the sheet of folded paper (see fig. 4.2). Doing this part of the fold correctly is important!

33

Third, fold the paper again from right to left, at an angle, making sure the edges of the fold are even as in figures 4.3 and 4.4.

Fourth, fold the left bottom edge of the paper under as in figure 4.4.

Fifth, at the proper moment, cut along the dotted lines as in figure 4.5. The actual size of the individual stars will be determined by the cut, line A to B (fig. 4.5). The farther up from the bottom point of the fold to B of the dotted line, the larger the bottom portion of the points of the star will be. (NOTE: The correct fold and cut of each star is critical if it is to have perfect form. So spend the time you need in practice until you can make each star correctly.)

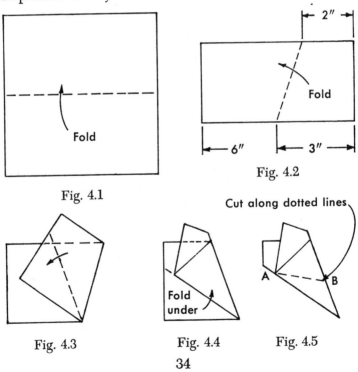

Fig. 4.1

Fig. 4.2

Fig. 4.3

Fig. 4.4

Fig. 4.5

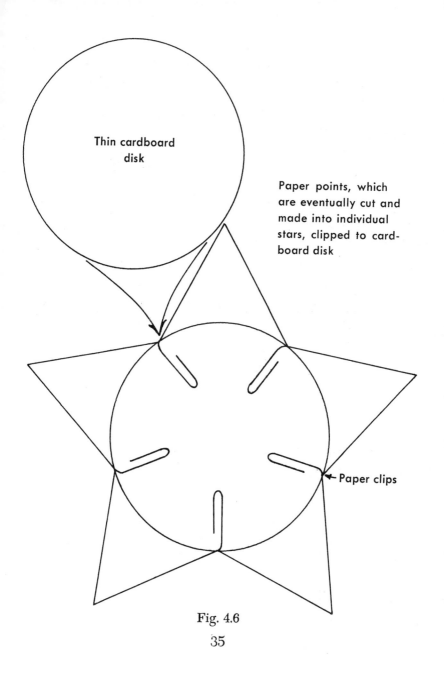

Thin cardboard disk

Paper points, which are eventually cut and made into individual stars, clipped to cardboard disk

Paper clips

Fig. 4.6

Message:

The Word of God says, "And they that be wise shall shine as the brightness of the firmament; and they that turn many to righteousness as the stars for ever and ever" (Dan. 12:3).

As true followers of Christ, we are to be ambassadors who witness for Him. We are to proclaim the good news that there is hope and salvation through faith in Jesus Christ our Lord. (*At this point you will show the cardboard disk and the five pieces of paper unfolded. Tell the group that the disk represents their church, Sunday school class, men's or women's group, etc.*)

As a local church or group of believers within the church, we are to shine as bright stars in the darkness of unbelief and sin in our community and world. Christ Himself gave our commission to us: "Go therefore and make disciples of all nations, baptizing them in the name of the Father and of the Son and of the Holy Spirit, teaching them to observe all that I have commanded you; and lo, I am with you always, to the close of the age" (Matt. 28:19-20, RSV).*

So let us form a large star from this disk by attaching five points from these five pieces of paper. Each of the points will represent a responsibility that you and I should assume in carrying out Christ's commission. (*As you state each of the five requirements, fold a sheet of paper into a point and clip it to the disk, thus forming a large star as shown in fig. 4.6.*)

Our first responsibility is to *go out* into the community to find those who are lost or who have strayed away from Christ's fold. (*Follow instructions in figs. 4.1 through 4.5 as you fold and clip the first point to the disk. Take as much time as you need to elaborate and illustrate this point.*)

*Revised Standard Version.

Next, we must *follow through* in our witness. We need to look for the right opportunity to present the good news of salvation and introduce Christ to them personally. (*Fold and clip the second point to the disk.*)

Then we must *confront unbelievers* with the claims of Christ. We must be bold, unafraid to present the truths of God's Word. We need to confront them with their sinful condition and their need of God's forgiveness through faith in Jesus Christ. Let them know of your concern for their spiritual welfare. Through your love they will sense Christ's spirit of forgiving love. The Holy Spirit is the one who will convict them of sin and woo them to a personal encounter with Christ. We are but the instruments through whom He works. (*Fold and clip the third point to the disk.*)

Next, we must *win them* to Christ and His church. We must be very careful here. We do not actually do the winning of men to Christ. This is the work of the Holy Spirit. Our task is to present the plan of salvation and be sure that they fully comprehend what is expected of them if they are to be born again, or have a conversion experience. We are not to push people into making a commitment. Our ministry is to sow the seed and water it; to reap is the work of the Holy Spirit. (*Fold and clip the fourth point to the disk.*)

Finally, we are responsible to *feed new believers*. Once an individual has accepted Christ, we are responsible to see that he or she is spiritually fed so that the process of maturing in Christ takes place. We have not fulfilled our Christian responsibility until we have taught those whom we have been instrumental in bringing to Christ to be disciples who feel responsible for winning others. (*Fold fifth point and clip to disk.*)

If we are faithful in our task of witnessing, we will soon see the results of our labors, for there will be numerous other stars shining as witnesses for Christ. Their light will help break through the darkness caused by sin and will bring hope to those who desperately need Christ as their personal Savior so as to have the assurance of the forgiveness of sins.

Many people think that there is just one large star, representing the corporate body of believers in Christ. But this is not true. Each follower of Jesus Christ must be a star shining in the darkness of sin. As each believer does his task faithfully, the entire body of saints will make its impact on the community and on the world. (*Take off the points of the large star, one at a time, and cut along line A-B on each folded piece of paper as in fig. 4.5. Unfold each piece of paper and show your audience the individual stars that have been produced from the points of the large star.*)

Elaborate on the importance of every person within the Body of Christ doing his share in winning others to Jesus as their Savior and Lord. In this way, the corporate Body of Christ will continue to grow, not only in numbers, but in the true spirit of Christ.

Other passages of Scripture you may wish to refer to are: Matthew 24:14; Luke 24:46-48; Acts 8:4-8; 10:34-43; 13:26-31; Romans 10:12-15; 1 Corinthians 1:17-18; 9:16-18; 15:11; 2 Corinthians 5:17-20; 2 Timothy 2:1-3; 4:2-8; and 1 John 5:8-15.

5

The Star of Bethlehem

(Matt. 2:1-12)

Materials Needed:

One 8½″×11″ sheet of paper or newspaper
One pencil
One pair of sharp scissors

Instructions for Paper Fold and Cut:

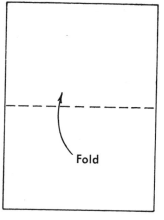

Fig. 5.1

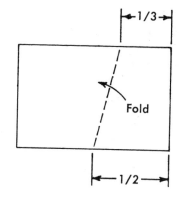

Fig. 5.2

39

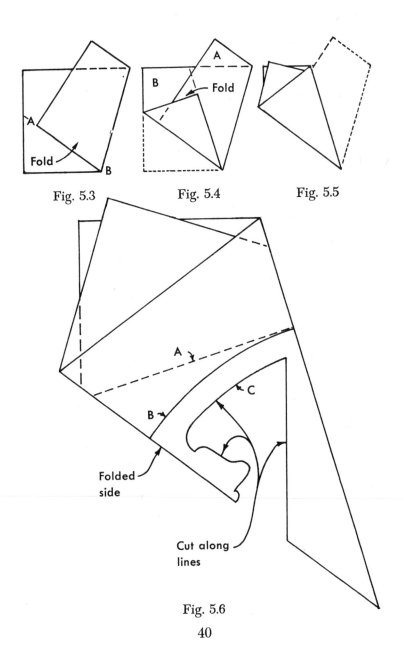

Fig. 5.3 Fig. 5.4 Fig. 5.5

A
B
Fold
C
Folded side
Cut along lines

Fig. 5.6

40

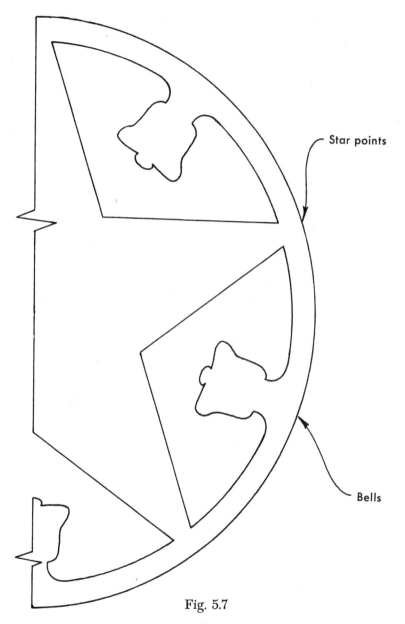

Star points

Bells

Fig. 5.7

41

First, fold the sheet of paper in half as in figures 5.1 and 5.2. Mark the center of the folded edge (see fig. 5.2).

Second, fold the right side over so that the top edge of the angle, which is to be formed, is one-third the length of the paper from the right edge, and the bottom edge of the angle is at the center of the paper (see figs. 5.2 and 5.3).

Third, fold up the left bottom corner of the paper on top of the paper forming an angle. Make sure that the bottom fold is tight against the fold A-B (see fig. 5.3). It should appear as it does in figure 5.4.

Fourth, fold side A on top of side B (see fig. 5.5). Make sure that the outer edges of the folded side are even (see fig. 5.6).

Fifth, outline lightly with a pencil on the sheet of folded paper the pattern to be cut out, as in figure 5.6. It is important that you check the position of the lowest piece of the fold, which is on the inside of the folded piece of paper (see A, fig. 5.6). This is essential in order to determine where the top line of the circle of the star should be traced (see B, fig. 5.6). Be sure that the circular lower line (see C, fig. 5.6), which will be cut from the bell toward the outer edge, is kept within one-quarter of an inch from the outer edge to the angled cut; otherwise the star points will not touch the circle edge as in figure 5.7.

Sixth, cut out the pattern you have outlined as in figure 5.6.

Seventh, open up the folded paper to show a five-pointed-star with five bells between the star points (see half view in fig. 5.7).

Message:

Read carefully the story of the birth of Jesus Christ as

recorded in Matthew 2:1-12 and Luke 2:1-20. You may use this paper folding and cutting message at any time of the year, but it is especially effective during the Christmas season.

Begin your message by relating the beautiful story of the birth of Christ as recorded by Luke. Relate how Joseph and Mary had to make the journey to Bethlehem, the city of David, in order to register for the census being conducted by Caesar Augustus. This trip was necessary because Joseph "was of the house and lineage of David" (Luke 2:4). Mary was about to give birth to her firstborn son, who was to be named Immanuel, "God with us" (Matt. 1:23).

As time permits, give the details of Jesus' birth: the announcement by an angel of the Lord to a group of shepherds in a field outside Bethlehem (Luke 2:8-12) and the angelic chorus "praising God and saying, 'Glory to God in the highest and on earth peace among men in His favor'" (Luke 2:13-14, MLB).* *As you are telling this portion of the story, begin to fold the sheet of paper as in figs. 5.1 through 5.5).*

Relate the story of the wise men as recorded in Matthew's gospel. Tell how they saw a star in the East and followed it (2:1-12). Give as many details as you wish. (*Then cut the outline traced on the folded sheet of paper, see fig. 5.6. Open the folded paper and show the star and five bells.*)

At this point, you may tell your audience how the star reminds us of God's special gift to the world, His only Son, Jesus Christ. God sent His Son into the world to demonstrate His great love for us, sinful though we may be, and to provide a way whereby we could be reconciled to Him

*New Berkeley Version in Modern English (Modern Language Bible).

43

through faith. Relate how the star should remind us, as it did the wise men long ago, that we, too, can rejoice and be exceedingly happy because of our Saviour's birth that first Christmas morning.

Refer to the five bells. They remind us of the angelic chorus and that we should experience beautiful music in our souls because we have personally acknowledged Christ as our Savior and Lord.

If you are giving this message at Christmas, tell how the star and bells have become symbols of the Christmas season, for it is a time of joy, happiness, and gaiety. However, we need to be very careful that, in the midst of all the Christmas festivities, we do not forget whose birthday we are celebrating. So as we hear the church bells and the beautiful songs of praise honoring Christ, this star with its surrounding bells should be a graphic reminder to us of the Savior's birth and the true meaning of Christmas.

You may conclude by saying: "May you rejoice in your salvation, and may your heart sing out, as did the angelic chorus that first Christmas, 'Glory to God in the highest and on earth peace among men in His favor'" (Luke 2:14, MLB).

Other passages of Scripture you may wish to refer to are: Genesis 3:15; Isaiah 7:14; 9:6; 11:1; Jeremiah 23:5; Micah 5:2-3; Luke 1:26-38; John 1:1-2; 1:14; 7:42; Acts 13:23; Romans 1:3; Galatians 3:16; 4:4; Philippians 2:7-8; Hebrews 7:16, 24-25; and Revelation 22:16.

6

Christ, Our Lighthouse of Hope

(Gospel song: "Brightly Beams Our Father's Mercy")

Materials Needed:

One sheet of typewriter paper or colored construction
paper, approximately 8½"×10"
One pencil
One pair of sharp scissors

Instructions for Paper Fold and Cut:

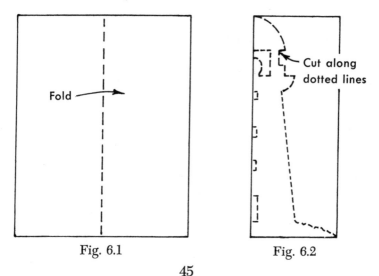

Fig. 6.1   Fig. 6.2

Fig. 6.3

First, fold the sheet of paper in half lengthwise (see figs. 6.1 and 6.2).

Second, draw the half-pattern of the lighthouse lightly with pencil, as your guide for cutting it out. Be sure to draw the pattern from the folded edge of the paper (see fig. 6.2).

Third, at the appropriate time during the message, cut along the pattern of the lighthouse, being sure to cut on all the dotted lines as in figure 6.2.

Fourth, unfold the paper and show the lighthouse to your audience.

Message:

Begin your message by stating that certain things are absolutely essential for the captain of a ship to know if he is to reach his destination safely. He must be very familiar with navigational charts and instruments, buoys that mark harbor channels and/or wrecked ships, and important landmarks along the shoreline. These are his guides, and he must rely heavily upon them. If he does not, he runs a great risk of having a shipwreck or running aground on a reef or sandbar.

Through the years, the lighthouse has been a tremendously important navigational landmark. It can be seen from a great distance during both the daylight hours and at night. The mariner steers toward it so he will reach the safety of the harbor on a stormy night. But it is the "lower lights" that warn him of individual rocks and reefs.

One gospel songwriter, Philip P. Bliss, used the lighthouse to teach spiritual truths when he wrote the familiar song, "Let the Lower Lights Be Burning." This gospel song portrays sinners as seamen lost in the stormy sea of sin and despair, but who are longing, hoping, and searching for a harbor of safety. Therefore, those of us who have been entrusted with the responsibility of being spiritual lower lights need to be sure that our lights are burning brightly at all times. We need to be constantly trimming the lamp so that lost seamen being tossed about in the stormy sea of life will be able to be guided into the safety of the harbor of Christ. (*At this point, you may wish the group to sing the gospel song "Let the Lower Lights Be Burning," or you may wish to wait and sing it at the conclusion of the message. I have found it very effective to have the group sing the various stanzas, one at a time, at appropriate places throughout the message.*)

If you wish to make this object lesson into a full sermon, rather than just a short introduction to the song, point out to your listeners some characteristics that will make them good landmarks to those who are lost.

The first characteristic is *courage*. Christians who want

to be witnesses for Christ must be courageous enough to confront the unsaved with their lost condition and their need of the saving grace of Jesus. They must explain carefully the plan of salvation as set forth in the Bible and make sure that the unbelievers comprehend its meaning.

The second characteristic is *faithfulness in Bible study.* The study of the Bible regularly and thoroughly is a must. Christians should be able to use the Bible in such a manner that unsaved people will observe that they are familiar with it and consider it tremendously important in their lives.

The third characteristic is *consistency in prayer.* Believers who are used by the Holy Spirit to help others must wait upon His guidance. The Holy Spirit is the One who convicts of sin and motivates lost individuals to place their faith in Jesus Christ as Savior and Lord. Prayer for His leadership is tremendously important.

The fourth characteristic is *consecration.* To be effective in soul winning, it is vital that Christians bear the fruit of the Spirit before those who need Christ (see Gal. 5:22-23). As they reveal Christ's love and values in their lives, they become guides to the safety of the harbor.

The fifth is *sincerity.* Effective witnesses for Christ must be sincere in their compassion for the people to whom they are proclaiming the gospel. It is important to remember that those to whom we witness can quickly discern whether or not they are really cared about as individuals and whether or not there is true concern for their spiritual welfare.

The sixth is the *ability to encourage.* Sincere Christians will encourage unbelievers to share in the community of saints. They will go and get them, if necessary, so that they can experience the warmth within the fellowship of a local church. This gives the Holy Spirit opportunities to urge them to make their public profession of faith in Jesus Christ and become a part of the community of saints. As active participants in the church, they will be helped to grow toward spiritual maturity.

You may wish to state some of the characteristics of Christians that tend to make them very poor landmarks with the result that the lost indeed become shipwrecked. I will not go into detail, but a listing of some of these negative characteristics may help you in developing this part of your message.

First is *disobedience to the call of Christ* to be faithful witnesses for Him wherever we are (see Acts 26:19-32 for an example of faithful witness).

Second is *self-centeredness*. It is very easy for individuals or churches to become so wrapped up in their own needs, concerns, and welfare that they lose sight of their mission and calling.

Third is *laziness*—just not being willing to expend the time and energy required to do the work of Christ.

Fourth is *spiritual backsliding.* A good example to use here would be that of Demas, as recorded in 2 Timothy 4:10.

Fifth is *procrastination*—putting off until tomorrow, or a more convenient season, what we know needs to be done immediately to spread the good news.

Other ideas will come to mind as you develop this portion of your message.

The main emphasis of this message is the urgent need for believers to give forth strong, bright beams of witness to the message of hope and salvation.

If you do not wish to use this fold and cut message as presented, you may develop a sermon based on Philippians

2:12-16, placing emphasis on our need to be constantly aware that God is at work in us seeking to carry out His will for our lives. We should be willing to do His will without grumbling, complaining, or questioning. Stress the point that He wills us to "Shine as lights in the world; holding forth the Word of life; that I may rejoice in the day of Christ, that I have not run in vain, neither laboured in vain" (Phil. 2:15*b*-16).

Other Scripture passages you may wish to refer to are: Psalm 119:11; Ephesians 6:6-8; Philippians 1:14, 27; Colossians 3:16-17; 2 Timothy 1:7; 4:2; and 1 John 2:4-6, 17.

7

God's Time Is Important

(Rom. 5:6)

Materials Needed:

One sheet of typewriter or construction paper, approximately 8½″×11″
One pair of scissors
One pencil
One black felt pen (optional)

Instructions for Paper Fold and Cut:

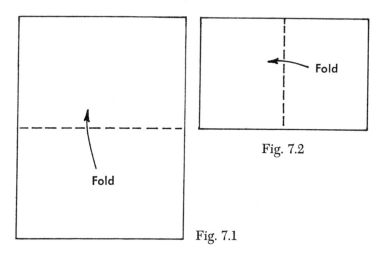

Fold

Fig. 7.1

Fold

Fig. 7.2

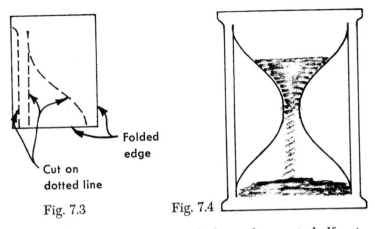

Folded
edge

Cut on
dotted line

Fig. 7.3   Fig. 7.4

First, fold the 8½-by-11-inch sheet of paper in half as in figure 7.1.

Second, fold the paper again into fourths as in figure 7.2.

Third, with a pencil lightly draw the hourglass outline on the paper as in figure 7.3. Be sure to note the position of the pattern in relation to the folded edges. If the pattern of the quarter portion of the hourglass is not positioned as shown in figure 7.3, the paper will not unfold into a complete hourglass as shown in figure 7.4.

Fourth, if you wish, use a black felt pen to draw the sand pouring through the hourglass as in figure 7.4.

Message:

People have always been interested in time. Down through the ages man has devised various instruments to assist him in keeping track of it.

The sun dial, introduced into Europe from the East, was an instrument that indicated the time of day by the sun's shadow thrown on a marked area. Later, the Chinese developed the water clock, a mechanism that measured time by the fall or flow of water. Then clocks were invented that worked on the principle of weights and springs. About 1000 A.D. a student at Cordova University added a pendulum, which made the existing clocks more accurate. Finally electric motors became the main source of energy moving the clocks' mechanisms. (*While you are talking, fold the paper with the pattern side facing you.*)

One ancient instrument that was used for the purpose of keeping time is still used today. Probably many of you have an hourglass in your kitchen where it is used to time a three-minute egg. Larger hourglasses are available for measuring longer periods of time.

An hourglass is one way we can see time passing, for as the sand slowly dribbles from the top of the hourglass, through the center, to the bottom, we realize that a certain amount of time has passed and is gone forever. (*At this point, cut out the pattern of the hourglass, unfold the paper, and show the hourglass to the audience.*)

The hourglass and all other timepieces—watches, mantel, grandfather, or modern digital clocks—are constant reminders to us that time, once passed, can never be brought back again; it is gone forever. Therefore, we need to use it wisely in the doing of God's will for our lives.

The Bible, God's eternal and inspired Word, has much to say about the importance of spending our time for the glory of God. I would like to point out a few principles of God's revealed will to you today.

At this point in the message, develop what you wish to teach about the importance of time. Here are passages of Scripture I have used effectively as a starting point for various talks given about how God wants us to use our time.

I have often used Romans 5:6 to point out God's timetable for providing our perfect salvation. I begin by telling of the Fall of man in the Garden of Eden and relate how God immediately set in motion a plan of redemption whereby mankind could be reconciled to Himself. Next, I explain what Paul meant when he wrote in Romans 5:6, "at the proper time," God sent His Son, Jesus Christ, into the world to die on Calvary to pay the penalty for our sins.

You may also use 2 Corinthians 6:2 as a basis for insisting that today, not tomorrow, is the right time to accept Christ as Savior and Lord. Emphasize the urgency of making a public commitment to Christ now, pointing out that tomorrow could be too late!

Romans 13:11-14 is a passage applicable to both believers and unbelievers. "Observe . . . the hour has struck for us to wake up. . . . The night is well advanced and the day approaches . . . clothe yourselves with the Lord Jesus Christ" (MLB). This entire passage lends itself to speaking on the importance of time as a factor in both the acceptance of Jesus Christ and in the urgency His followers should feel in proclaiming the gospel.

Last, you may wish to use Ephesians 5:15-17 to emphasize the importance of wise conduct, believers being sure that they are making the best possible use of their time in the work of the Lord. Stress the importance of daily prayer, Bible study, and meditation so they will gain the needed insights to know the will of God for their lives.

As you have noted, the subject of time can be developed in many ways or directions. It can be the basis of an evangelistic appeal or a challenge to believers to use their time wisely.

Other appropriate passages of Scripture are: 1 Corinthians 4:5; Galatians 4:1-10, 21-31; Colossians 4:2-6; 2 Thessalonians 2:1-17; 2 Timothy 4:1-5; Hebrews 9:27; James 4:14; Revelation 1:3; 12:12.

8

The Indestructible Book

(*Luke* 21:33)

Materials Needed:

Two 3″×12″ strips of thin paper having the word *BIBLE* printed in large letters on each piece
A black felt pen or large print press-on lettering
A tube of glue or paste (Rubber glue is best.)

Instructions for Paper Fold and Tear:

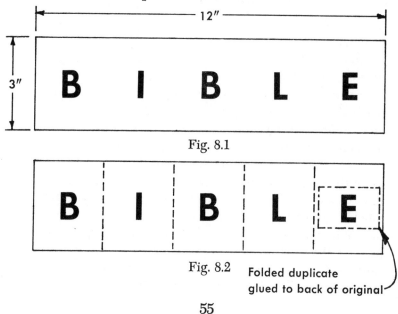

Fig. 8.1

Fig. 8.2   **Folded duplicate glued to back of original**

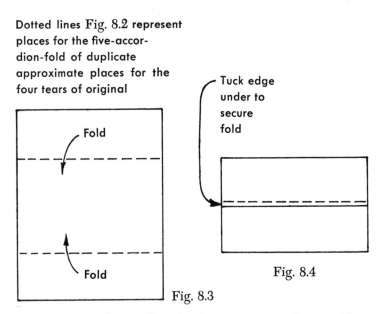

Dotted lines Fig. 8.2 represent places for the five-accordion-fold of duplicate approximate places for the four tears of original

Fold

Fold

Fig. 8.3

Tuck edge under to secure fold

Fig. 8.4

First, print the word *BIBLE* on two strips of paper identical in size, color, and thickness. Be sure that the printing is identical. You can use either a felt pen or large-print press-on lettering.

Second, fold one of the strips into a small, neat piece of paper as in figures 8.3 and 8.4 and glue it to the back of the other strip (see fig. 8.2). Check to make sure that this duplicate piece of paper is glued in the correct position so that when it is opened out, the word *BIBLE* will appear as on the original strip. Also make sure that the fold (see figs. 8.3 and 8.4) is done correctly so that the strip can be quickly and easily opened at the proper time. It is important that you make a few of these strips ahead of time and practice the tearing of the original strip at the appropriate time, and opening of the duplicate to make sure that you are making and using the strips correctly.

Third, tear the original piece of paper into five pieces. Place the pieces on top of each other and fold them into a small packet in the palm of your hand. This packet should be folded so that it is similar in size to the duplicate piece glued to the original.

Fourth, at the proper time, turn the paper over and open up the duplicate strip, showing that the torn paper has been "restored."

Note: The duplicate piece of paper should be folded accordion style. Fold down the top edge to the center (see fig. 8.3). Then fold the bottom part of the paper toward the center just far enough to tuck the edge under the upper fold in order to hold it in place (see fig. 8.4). Be sure to glue securely the back portion of the fold in the proper position to the back of the original (see fig. 8.2). The duplicate piece of paper should be glued on the left side of the original when the letters are facing the audience. This way the duplicate will be covered by the fingers of your left hand. The same will be true of the torn pieces of the original. When the piece of paper is shown "restored," simply wad up the original and place it in your pocket or anywhere out of sight.

Message:

Begin your message by reading Luke 21:33. Show the piece of paper with the word *BIBLE* printed on it. Tell your audience that this piece of paper represents the Bible, God's eternal, indestructible Word. Go into detail about how the Bible was inspired of God and is His progressive revelation of Himself to mankind. His final revelation came in the incarnation of His Son, Jesus Christ. You may wish to give illustrations from the Bible of how wonderful God's

Word is, and how it presents the good news of salvation to all mankind.

Mention that all people do not regard the Bible as the inspired Word of God. Emphasize how Satan and his followers, down through the ages, have done everything within their power to destroy the Bible, or to minimize its influence by declaring that it is nothing more than a book of religious thought and is not relevant to our time. Illustrate from history how the Bible, in spite of diabolic attacks, has survived. (*Stress this important point by tearing the original strip of paper into small pieces, thus illustrating how Satan and his followers have sought, by every devious means possible, to destroy the Bible and its influence on the lives of individuals and the world at large. Keep the duplicate strip folded out of sight in your hand.*)

Tell how, to the amazement of many people, the Bible has been indestructible; in fact, it remains today the best seller among books and retains its tremendous power to change people's lives. (*Unfold the paper in your hand to illustrate how, in spite of Satan's attacks, the Bible is still whole and retains its power to make an impact on the lives of people.*)

State that, according to the Word of God, the Bible can and will withstand any efforts to destroy it or to make it nonrelevant in any age, including our own. The following illustrations emphasize this essential truth.

In the middle of the nineteenth century, Felix Risenberg was stationed aboard *St. Mary's of Hellsgate*, the ship that patrolled the dangerous pass in the East River between Manhattan Island and Long Island, called Hell Gate. One day he received a package from home, and not wanting the food in it to be consumed by his shipmates, he decided to hide it in a safe place. In the ship's library he found an unused closet with fifty old, dusty Bibles stored on its shelves. Thinking this to be a perfect hiding place for his food package, he dropped the Bibles, one by one, through the porthole.

Some minutes later, the captain of the ship came rushing into the library and demanded that the young librarian tell him what was going on: "There are fifty Bibles flowing with the tide through Hell's Gate, and I want an explanation!"

The young librarian finally got up enough courage to answer, "Well, sir, I threw them through the porthole. I'm sorry, but I thought they would sink."

Many other people have thought the Bible was a sinkable Book. Voltaire, a vocal eighteenth-century infidel, believed it was. He once said that one hundred years from the date upon which he was speaking, the Bible would cease to be read and would be seen only in museums. But one hundred years from that date, the very place where Voltaire had stood when he made the statement was one of the distribution points for the Bible Society. And at that time all of Voltaire's ninety-two works went on sale. The first editions were purchased by the Earl of Dunedine for one cent a copy, while on that same day a man purchased a copy of the Gutenberg Bible for $175,000 and presented it to the Yale University library.

Not only is the Bible still the world's best seller, but just recently members of the Micrometrology Laboratories Firm of Texas built a Bible which is the smallest in the world. It was made at the cost of $65,000 and took modern technology six years to achieve this feat. The August 1977 issue of *Popular Science Magazine* stated: "Every page of the King James Bible was reduced to a rectangle only 0.02 inch by 0.012 inch. . . . The pages are arrayed on the tiny glass chip in rows of fifty pages across and thirty-one pages deep; they can be read only with a 300-power microscope."

Do you know of any other book on which a firm would spend so much time, energy, technology, and money in order to reduce it in size?

So, you see, the old Book still stands, and it is still powerful and relevant. All we have to do is read it, believe it, and allow the Holy Spirit to enable us to live by its teachings. Jesus said, "Heaven and earth shall pass away: but my words shall not pass away" (Luke 21:33).

Other passages of Scripture you may wish to use are: Philippians 2:13-16; 2 Timothy 3:16; 4:1-5; Titus 1:9-16; 1 Peter 1:22-25; 2 Peter 1:19-21; 1 John 2:5; and Revelation 3:8; 22:19.

9

Jacob's Ladder

(Gen. 28:10-22)

Materials Needed:

Three double sheets of newspaper (blank newsprint
from a printer preferred over regular newspaper sheets
with pictures and print on them)
A sharp knife, if paper is too tough to tear
Two small rubber bands

Instructions for Fold and Cut or Tear:

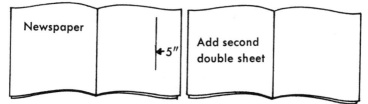

Fig. 9.1

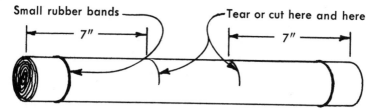

Fig. 9.2

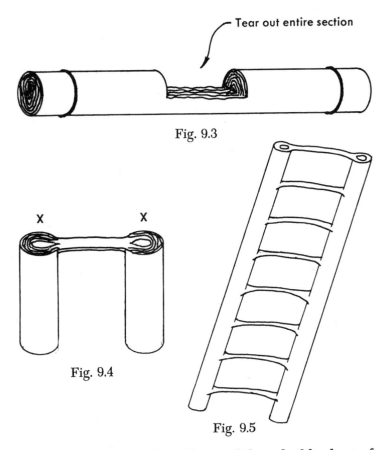

Tear out entire section

Fig. 9.3

X   X

Fig. 9.4

Fig. 9.5

First, make a tube by rolling tightly a double sheet of newspaper. When you are approximately five inches from the edge, add another double-page sheet (see fig. 9.1). Keep on rolling the newspaper; then add the third sheet in the same manner as the second. Be sure to roll the newspaper toward you so you can keep the roll tight. Periodically, tap the ends of the roll in order to keep the edges even. Place a small rubber band on each end to keep the roll tight until you are ready to use it (see fig. 9.2).

Second, flatten the tube to make it easier to work with. When you are ready for the tear, be sure to use the measurements shown in figure 9.2. Tear or cut through the tube twice as in figure 9.2. Please note the proportion of the cuts or tears so that you leave intact a horizontal strip between the two. Next, tear out the part between the two tears as shown in figure 9.3.

Third, bend the ends of the torn tube down at right angles to the center part (see fig. 9.4). Be very careful that you do not tear off any of the center strips.

Fourth, this move is the most difficult one. Remove the rubber bands and ask an assistant to hold the lower ends of the tube as you extend the ladder. Insert a finger in each tube at the Xs (see fig. 9.4). Draw the ends upward slowly, forming a beautiful ladder. Small children especially love this paper effect. As the paper stretches upward, the ladder gradually takes on an amazing lifelike appearance. Be sure to practice this effect before using it.

Message:

(*NOTE: The roll of paper that you will use for making the ladder should be prepared in advance and placed on some object in clear view of the audience during the telling of the story. However, do not draw attention to it until the proper moment in the message.*)

To prepare for this message, read Genesis 26-28. These chapters will give you information about God's confirmation of the Abrahamic covenant to Isaac and the birth of his twin sons Jacob and Esau.

Tell your audience the background of Jacob and Esau. Although twins, Esau was the first born, therefore, the elder son. According to tradition, Esau was entitled to his

63

father's possessions plus a special blessing before Isaac died (Gen. 27:1-4).

Esau was an outdoorsman who loved to hunt, farm, and work with his hands. He was his father's favorite son (Gen. 25:27). Jacob, on the other hand, preferred to stay around the house and he became the favorite son of his mother, Rebekah (Gen. 25:28).

Give the details of Isaac's request that Esau hunt for some venison to make him a savoury meal to eat before he died. After the meal Isaac was going to bestow upon Esau the special blessing (Gen. 27:1-4).

Rebekah overheard her husband's conversation with their oldest son. And because of her great love for Jacob, she wanted him to receive the blessing instead of his brother, Esau. Therefore, she devised a plot to disguise Jacob, and thus deceive Isaac into thinking he was Esau. She knew that Isaac was blind, and the only way that he could be sure of Esau's identity was by feeling his hairy hands and smelling the clothes that he wore. So she cooked a meal for Jacob to take to his father, put some hairy goat skins on his hand, and dressed him in his brother's clothes. She then sent him to his father Isaac. At first, Isaac was not sure that the son before him was Esau. The voice was that of Jacob; to be certain of his identity, Isaac had the imposter come close so he could feel his hands. Because of the hairy goatskin, Jacob's smooth hands felt like Esau's hairy ones. So Isaac was tricked into believing that Jacob was Esau, and he gave him the blessing (Gen. 27:8-29).

When Esau finally returned with the venison, he was too late. Isaac had already given the blessing to his brother Jacob and could not take it back. Esau became very angry because of the deception and planned to take his brother's life (Gen. 27:41). When Rebekah heard of

Esau's plans, she hurriedly sent Jacob away to her brother Laban's house at Haran (Gen. 27:41-45). After traveling a full day's journey, Jacob, tired and lonely, lay down on the hard ground with only a stone for a pillow. As he slept, he dreamed he saw a ladder standing on the ground and stretching all the way to heaven. Angels were ascending and descending upon it, and at the top of it stood the Lord God of Abraham. God assured Jacob that the blessing he had received was that which had been given to his father Abraham. Then He promised Jacob, "Behold, I am with you and will keep you wherever you go, and will bring you back to this land; for I will not leave you until I have done that of which I have spoken to you" (28:15, RSV).

(During this portion of your message, cut or tear the center part of the paper and, with the help of an assistant, slowly open it out making the ladder [figs. 9.3-9.5]).

Conclude by telling how Jacob awoke from his sleep and acknowledged that the Lord was truly with him. He took the stone, which had been his pillow, and set it up as a memorial. He named the place Bethel, the house of God, and there Jacob made a sacred vow to God. This experience became a turning point in his life (Gen. 28:20-22).

You may wish to make a practical application of the story. For example, point out that God is not confined to any one place or building, but that He is everywhere. Or you may deal with the importance of keeping one's vows to God. Use your own experiences and creativity in making the application.

Other Scripture passages you may wish to refer to are: Genesis 9:12-16; 17:1-8, 19-21; Exodus 34:1-10; 1 Chronicles 11:3; 2 Chronicles 21:7; Jeremiah 11:1-5; Acts 3:25; Galatians 3:15-29; Ephesians 2:11-22; and Hebrews 8:1-13; 12:24.

10

Making "I" Too Important in Life

(*Gen. 28–35:15*)

Materials Needed:

One 5″×24″ sheet of paper (stiff if available)
One pair of scissors
One pencil
One ruler

Instructions for Paper Fold and Cut:

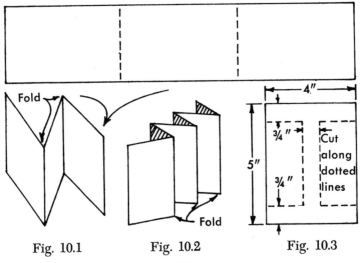

Fig. 10.1   Fig. 10.2   Fig. 10.3

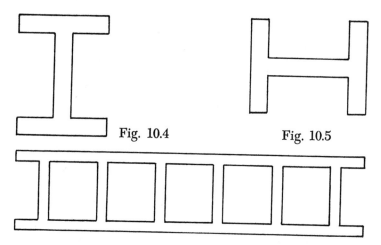

Fig. 10.4

Fig. 10.5

Fig. 10.6

First, fold the strip of paper into three equal parts making an accordion fold (see fig. 10.1).

Second, fold the paper into sixths, making an accordion fold (see fig. 10.2).

Third, draw the pattern on the end of the accordion fold as in figure 10.3. Be sure that you use dimensions given in the instructions.

Fourth, cut along the dotted lines of the pattern, holding the folded paper tightly together, as you cut. (This should be done at the proper time during the message.) When the paper is cut, it will form the letter *I* (see fig. 10.4).

Fifth, at the proper time, turn the piece of paper on one side. It will then form the letter *H* (see fig. 10.5).

Sixth, at the proper time, unfold the piece of paper to form a ladder (see fig. 10.6).

Message:

You may use this message by itself, or as a follow-up to "Jacob's Ladder," chapter nine. However, this one emphasizes Jacob's self-centeredness and the consequences he suffered.

Tell the group that because of Jacob's eagerness to follow his mother Rebekah's instructions (Gen. 27:6-19), he allowed the "I" in his life to take precedence over his love for his brother Esau. Jacob was determined to receive the blessing from his father regardless of the deception involved in getting it. He wanted for himself what rightly belonged to his older brother Esau, even though Esau, in a moment of weakness and hunger, had sold his birthright to Jacob for a bowl of lentil stew (Gen. 25:29-34). (*Fold the strip of paper as in figs. 10.1, 10.2, and 10.3 and cut out the pattern.*)

Show the letter *I*, and note how tragic it is when people put themselves first in life regardless of whom they may hurt. When "I" becomes the essential motivator in people's lives, they are headed for trouble. Point out how easily me-first people rationalize their actions, but ultimately the only people they are deceiving are themselves.

You may wish to use either personal, biographical, or biblical illustrations to emphasize this essential truth. Some biblical examples are: David (2 Sam. 11-12); Achan (Josh. 7); and Jonah (Jonah 1-4).

Resume telling Jacob's story. State that as a result of Jacob's putting himself first, he had to suffer certain consequences. He had to leave home and travel across a lonely, desolate country. He was afraid of what Esau might do to him because he had cheated him out of his birthright. He had to live with deep feelings of guilt because he had deceived his father. He was deceived by Laban, then had to work long, hard years for him in order to marry Rachel (Gen. 29). Eventually, even his family suffered as a result of his sin (Gen. 31). Go into detail as to how putting self first in one's life is a sin that affects not only the life of the person who commits it, but also has adverse effects on family, close friends, and others. Tell of God's way out for trapped me-first people by relating how Jacob finally recalled the covenant he had made with God when he first fled from home (Gen. 28:20-22).

(*Turn the paper on one side and show the letter* H). Say that God is always available to us through prayer. He loves us and only waits for us to turn to Him so He can help us. (*To illustrate Jacob's experience at the city of Luz [Gen. 28:11-22] unfold the paper and show the ladder as you remind the group of Jacob's dream on this important occasion in his life years before, of his vow to God, and of his eventual return to Bethel [Gen. 35:1-4].*)

Conclude by telling of Jacob's reunion with his brother Esau (Gen. 33). Relate how Jacob, following the tragic events recorded in Genesis 34, recalled his Bethel experience, repented of his sins, and returned to Bethel. There God appeared to him again and blessed him. It was at this time that his name was changed from Jacob, the underhanded, to Israel, a prince with God (Gen. 35:9-15).

Apply the truth of the message by mentioning God's forgiving love as revealed in Jesus Christ and His desire to see us reconciled to Himself through faith in Christ's atoning death on Calvary. Stress the importance of childlike faith in Jesus Christ as Savior and Lord, if one is to find forgiveness of sins and have the assurance that his name is written in the Lamb's book of life.

Other relevant passages of Scripture are: Acts 2:21; 15:11; 16:31; Romans 1:17; 3:21-26; 4:13-25; 10:13; 1 Corinthians 6:11; Galatians 2:16-21; 3:11; 3:15-22; Ephesians 2:5; 2:8-10; 4:32; Hebrews 8:6; 9:15-22; 12:22-24; Titus 3:5-8; and 1 John 1:9.

11

Anchored in the Safe Harbor of Christ

(*Heb. 6:19-20*)

Materials Needed:

One 8½″×11″ sheet of white or pastel-colored paper
One black felt pen or black press-on lettering
One pair of scissors
A piece of transparent tape
One pencil

Instructions for Paper Fold and Cut:

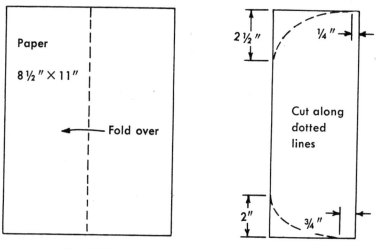

Fig. 11.1

Paper

8½″ × 11″

← Fold over

Fig. 11.2

2½″

¼″

Cut along dotted lines

2″

¾″

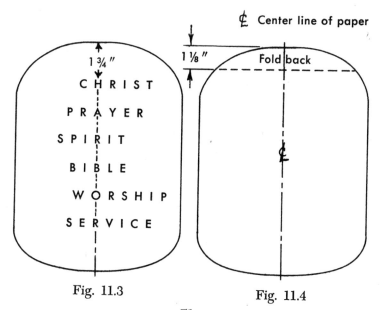

Fig. 11.3

1¾″

C H R I S T

P R A Y E R

S P I R I T

B I B L E

W O R S H I P

S E R V I C E

Fig. 11.4

₵ Center line of paper

1⅛″

Fold back

₵

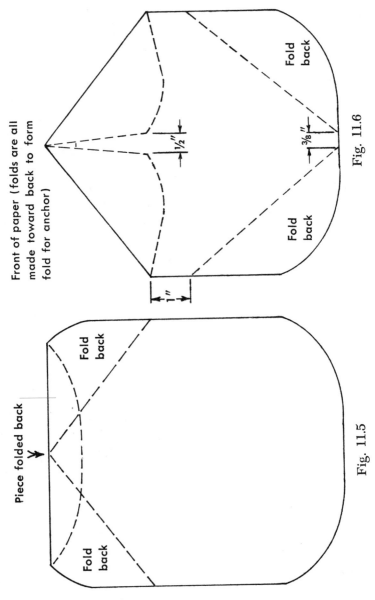

Front of paper (folds are all made toward back to form fold for anchor)

1/2"

3/8"

Fig. 11.6

1"

Piece folded back

Fold back

Fold back

Fold back

Fold back

Fig. 11.5

72

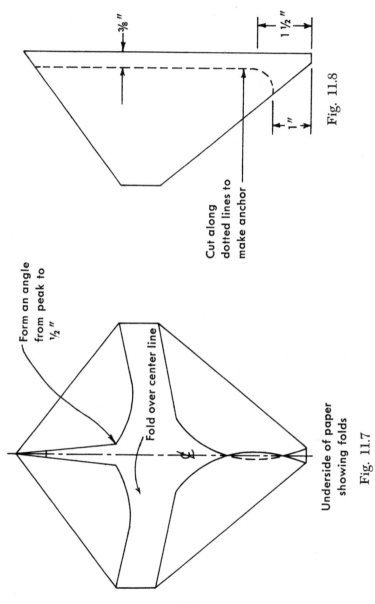

Form an angle from peak to ½"

Fold over center line

℄

Underside of paper showing folds

Fig. 11.7

3/8"

1 ½"

1"

Cut along dotted lines to make anchor

Fig. 11.8

73

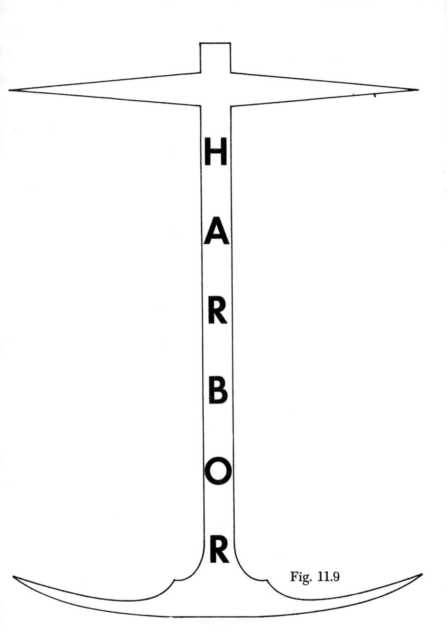

Fig. 11.9

First, fold an 8½-by-11-inch sheet of paper in half vertically (see fig. 11.1).

Second, draw with a pencil the pattern according to the dimensions shown in figure 11.2. You should do this prior to the presentation so the paper is ready for you to cut off the rounded edges at the proper time.

Third, cut off the edges and open the piece of paper. On the front side of the paper (the opposite side from where the folds will be made) print in large letters the six words shown in figure 11.3. Be sure that the letters that appear on the center line are spaced exactly on the line, as in figure 11.3. Special care should be taken to leave at least 1¾ inches of vertical space between the letter H and the top of the paper, as shown in figure 11.3. This is important, because when the paper is folded and cut to form the anchor, the letters should appear as in figure 11.9.

Fifth, fold back the top edge of the paper 1⅛ inches behind the printed side (see fig. 11.4).

Sixth, fold back the right and left upper corners to form an angle as in figures 11.5 and 11.6. Be sure the angle formed is such that there is a half inch separation between the upper corner folds as shown in figure 11.7.

Seventh, fold back the right and left lower corners of the paper as in figures 11.6 and 11.7. Note the measurements given in figure 11.7. It is important that the edges of the folds meet at the center line of the paper.

Eighth, fold the sheet of paper in half and cut along the dotted lines (see fig. 11.8). Note the measurements given in figure 11.8; they will help make a more perfectly formed anchor, as shown in figure 11.9.

Ninth, unfold the sheet of paper after it has been cut and you will have an anchor with the word *HARBOR* printed on it (see fig. 11.9).

Message:

This is a marvelous paper-fold-and-cut object lesson, which can be used for both children and adult audiences. It presents an evangelistic message. Anyone who wants to can have the inner peace that comes through knowing he is safe and secure in the harbor of Christ because he has accepted Christ as his Savior.

I usually start this message by referring to Paul's shipwreck experience recorded in Acts 27. After telling about the storm at sea, I refer to verse 29, "Then, for fear we might run aground on submerged rocks, they cast four anchors from the stern and longed for break of day" (MLB).

Then I ask how many have been through similar experience—not in the literal sense of actually being in a storm at sea, but from the viewpoint of feeling all was hopeless in a certain situation or set of circumstances in their lives. With fear and trembling, they had longed for daybreak to come, knowing that during the darkest hours they might be cast upon the rocks and shipwrecked in the storm of life.

Those who do not know Christ as their personal Savior do not possess the kind of anchor that will hold securely when the storms of life come. Millions of people have tried various types of anchors during life's storms, only to find that there was no safety or security in any of them. The writer of Hebrews tells us, "To this hope we anchor the soul safely and securely, and it reaches on beyond the veil into the Holy of Holies, where Jesus entered in for us in advance" (Heb. 6:19-20a, MLB).

I tell the group that I would like to discuss six proved anchors that will hold their souls safely and securely no matter how stormy life may become. For if they are securely anchored in Christ Jesus, they need have no fear of being dashed upon the rocks of uncertainty, failure, or defeat. These anchors will hold them fast until they make the safety of the harbor.

Take each of the six words listed on the sheet of paper (see fig. 11.4) and develop them through the use of scripture texts and biblical, historical, and personal illustrations. (*At this point fold the paper as in figures 11.1 and 11.2. Cut off the upper and lower edges of the paper along the dotted lines (see fig. 11.2). Hold up the paper, unfolded, with the printed words toward the audience and draw their attention to the six words. Tape the piece of paper to the front of the pulpit, chalkboard, or any surface that will keep the words visible to the audience while you are discussing each of them.*)

Develop each of the six words into the body of your message. The following ideas are merely suggestions as to how you might build a message around each of the words.

First, *CHRIST*—In order to have the assurance that you are saved from sin, you must personally, through faith, accept Christ as your Savior and Lord. You must have a personal encounter with Him. Here is an opportunity to present to your audience the basic plan of salvation in simple terms. Start with the fact that every person has sinned and fallen short of the glory of God (Rom. 3:23; Gal. 3:22-24; 1 John 1:10). Point out that it is impossible for any individual to find favor in the sight of God through any merit or works of his own. Salvation is freely given by God's grace to each believer and does not depend on any works of righteousness (Eph. 2:8-9; Titus 3:5-6). Tell how God can justify us through the redemptive plan He provided—He sent His only Son, Jesus Christ, to die on Calvary to atone for our sins (John 3:16-18). Stress the point that it is through faith in His atoning work that we are saved and reconciled to God.

Other passages of Scripture you may wish to use here are: Matthew 1:21; 18:11; Luke 18:19; John 5:24; 16:7-11; Acts 2:21; 4:12; 15:11; Romans 5:8; 6:23; 10:8-13; 1 Corinthians 15:3; 2 Corinthians 6:2; Galatians 3:21-29; Titus 3:1-8; 1 Peter 3:18; and 1 John 1:9-10.

Second, *PRAYER*—Point out the importance of prayer in the Christian life. Not only do we need to pray for the forgiveness of our sins and repent (make an about-face) of our sinful ways (Mark 6:12; Luke 13:3, 5; Acts 3:19; 17:30), but prayer must be a daily discipline if we are to live victorious lives in Christ. Through prayer, we communicate with Him who is the source of our spiritual strength and growth (Romans 12:1-2; Col. 4:2; 1 Thess. 5:17).

Other relevant passages of Scripture are: Proverbs 15:8; Matthew 21:22; Ephesians 1:15-21; 3:14-21; 6:10-18; Philippians 4:6-7; James 5:16; and Revelation 5:8-9.

Third, *THE HOLY SPIRIT*—Upon acceptance of Christ as personal Savior, the Holy Spirit comes into a believer's life to comfort, strengthen, and assist in the spiritual development of his new nature (John 14:16-26; Acts 1:8; Romans 5-6; 1 Cor. 3:16). Point out that the old nature is still present within believers, and we need the presence of the Holy Spirit in our lives so that we can be victorious over sin and the devil. However, the Holy Spirit, although present in our lives, will not force Himself upon us. We must allow Him to take control of our lives completely. And He must be in control if our old nature is to be subdued and our new nature is to bear the fruit of the Spirit. As we open up our lives to His leadership, He will fill us with His power, strength, courage, and peace. Through Him we become strong in the inner man and overcome the temptations of the evil one, Satan (Eph. 3:14-19).

Additional passages of Scripture concerning the Holy Spirit are: John 16:7-11; Acts 19:1-7; Romans 8:9-13; 15: 13, 16; 1 Corinthians 6:19-20; Galatians 3:13-14; 4:6-7; Ephesians 5:18; Titus 3:5; and 1 John 3:14.

Fourth *THE BIBLE*, God's eternal and inspired Word— The study of God's Word is an essential part of our growth toward spiritual maturity (1 Peter 2:2). We need to discipline ourselves to regularly and thoroughly feed upon the truths of the inspired Word of God. This is one of the chief means through which we can know God's will and grow in our desire to serve Him and to love our fellowman (Eph. 4:11-16). Through reading, studying, and meditating upon the Word of God, we learn how the Holy Spirit works within us to do the will of Christ. The Bible must be our spiritual guidebook and road map on our journey through life.

You may wish to study the following passages: Romans 1:16-17; 15:4; Colossians 3:16-17; 2 Timothy 2:15-17; 3: 15-17; 4:2; Titus 1:9; Hebrews 4:12-13; and 2 Peter 3:15-18.

Fifth, *WORSHIP*—As young Christians, we need the fellowship with other believers and God which is available to us through worship experiences within the church. When we truly worship God in spirit and in truth, He becomes our anchor which steadies us when the sea of life becomes stormy, and we need a haven of safety (John 4:23-24). We derive from worship of God and fellowship with the body of believers the spiritual uplift we need daily as we live the Christian life. Without worship and the fellowship and communion that is a part of it, we tend to drift back into the old life of sin. Thus, the church, with its worship and fellowship, is essential to the growth of our inner man so that our new nature will be victorious over our old nature

Study the following passages of Scripture as you develop this important theme: Romans 12:5; 1 Corinthians 12:12-26; 2 Corinthians 8:4; Galatians 3:26-29; Ephesians 2:19-22; 3:14-19; Philippians 1:3-6; Hebrews 10:25; and 1 John 1:3-7.

Sixth, *SERVICE* to Christ and to our fellowman—Christians who wish to mature spiritually must give of themselves through some form of Christian service. They must become more than just mere pew warmers. They are called of God, through Christ, to serve Him faithfully—to put their talents to work and to use their spiritual gifts in the spreading of the gospel. Those who are truly led of the Spirit of God will have a desire to use their gifts and talents for His glory. Believers do not work in order to merit salvation or earn favor in God's sight, but they serve God as they evidence their personal encounter with Christ, A faith that saves can be expected to manifest itself in service to Christ and His kingdom's work (James 2:14-20).

You may wish to refer to these additional Scriptures: Matthew 16:25; 28:16-20; Romans 12:1-8; 2 Corinthians 6:1; Galatians 5:16-25; 2 Timothy 1:9; Titus 2:7, 14; 3:5, 14; Hebrews 10:19-25; James 2:14, 18, 21-26; and Revelation 20:12.

(Fold the sheet of paper as shown in figures 11.4-11.8. Cut along the dotted line as in figure 11.8; then unfold the paper showing the anchor with the word HARBOR printed on it [see fig. 11.9]. The first few times you present this paper-fold-and-cut-message, you will find it easier if you fold the sheet of paper in advance, without cutting the edges as in figure 11.3. Mark with a pencil the dotted lines to be cut [see fig. 11.8]. After a few times you will auto-

matically know where to cut in order to make the anchor, as in figure 11.9.)

You may conclude your message by reading Hebrews 6:19-20 and explaining what Paul meant by the safety and security that is found through faith in Jesus Christ as Savior and Lord.

12

The Call to Be Disciples

(Matt. 8:19-22; Luke 9:23)

Materials Needed:

A 5″×20″ sheet of paper (two or more pieces of paper
may be taped or glued together)
A pair of scissors
A pencil

Instructions for Paper Fold and Cut:

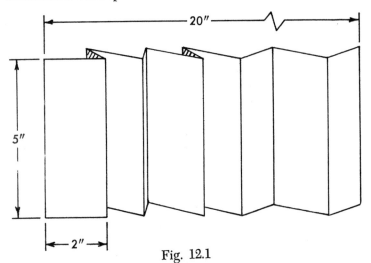

Fig. 12.1

Cut along lines

Fig. 12.2

Fig. 12.3

83

First, fold the sheet of paper accordion style as in figure 12.1. Be sure each of the folds is 2 inches wide.

Second, draw the pattern of a boy and a girl on the top section of the folded paper as in figure 12.2. Depending on your artistic ability, use the design shown or draw one of your own.

Third, at the appropriate moment in the message, hold the paper folds firmly together and, with a pair of sharp scissors, cut around the patterns of the boy and girl figures.

Fourth, at the right time in the message, slowly unfold the figures to display the row of boys and girls holding hands. When you are pulling the folded figures apart, be careful not to tear the thin strip of paper that joins them together into one long row of figures (see fig. 12.3).

Message:

Before presenting this object lesson, study carefully Genesis 6-7. Begin by relating how the human race, whom God had created and loved, had sinned to such a degree that He no longer could stand their rebellion and perversion. He, therefore, decided it would be best to destroy them, because their lust for power had grown so great (see Gen. 6:13, MLB).

However, among all of the world's sinful and depraved people, God saw one man who was upright and "blameless among his fellow men" (Gen. 6:9, MLB). So God told Noah His plan to destroy all His creation by sending a great flood to cover the earth. God instructed Noah to build an ark for the safety of himself and his family, plus pairs of all beasts and birds (Gen. 6:14-22). He also established a covenant with Noah that all those in the ark would be saved from the destruction caused by the flood.

Give as many details of the Flood, recorded in Genesis

7-8, as you wish. These would include: the destruction of all the human race except Noah and his family; the subsiding of the flood waters; the landing of the ark on Mount Ararat; Noah, his family, the animals, birds, and creeping things leaving the ark; Noah building an altar to the Lord in thanksgiving; and God's covenant "never again [to] curse the ground on man's account" (Gen. 8:21).

Tell how God down through the ages has sought to reveal to sinful people His great love for them and His desire for their reconciliation to Him. His final revelation came when He sent His only Son, Jesus Christ, to die on Calvary for their sins (John 3:16), that through faith in Christ's atoning work on the cross, all who believe can be saved and reconciled to God (John 5:24).

Mention that Noah warned the people of the coming judgment of God and extended to them an invitation to be saved by entering into the ark; now Christ has extended to each of us an invitation to be saved if we will believe in Him. The moment we trust Him, we will be saved and know the security of being in Christ's ark of safety (John 5:24; Rom. 3:21-26; 5:1-11).

Once we have accepted Christ as our pesronal Savior, we are called by Him to become His disciples and to follow Him. In the scope of the four gospels, Jesus' command, "Follow Me" is recorded some ten times. He told Peter and Andrew that if they would leave their fishing nets and follow Him, He would make them become fishers of men, a far more important task (Matt. 4:19).

On another occasion, a scribe expressed a desire to follow Him, but, when Christ told him what it might mean in sacrifice, he decided against being a disciple (Matt. 8:19-20). Another would-be disciple begged off by saying that he had to attend the burial of his father. Jesus felt His call to be so imperative that He commanded, "Follow Me, and let the dead bury their dead" (Matt. 8:21-22).

In the case of the rich young man who came to Jesus asking how he might inherit eternal life, Jesus' call to discipleship included cross-bearing. He said to this young man, "If you would be perfect, go, sell what you possess and give it to the poor . . . and come, follow me" (Matt. 19:16-21, RSV). But "He went away sorrowful" (Matt. 19:22), because the price was too great for him to pay.

On another occasion, Jesus said to all who were present, "If any man will come after me, let him deny himself, and take up his cross daily, and follow me" (Luke 9:23). Jesus' invitation to discipleship is given to all of us who claim to be His followers. We are expected to leave all and follow Him. His call is to a life of self-denial and cross-bearing.

The call to discipleship applies to all individuals, regardless of age, who truly wish to follow His commands. Christ had a deep love in His heart for children. One example of this love is recorded in Matthew 19:13-15. One day when Jesus was teaching the multitudes, a number of people on the outskirts of the crowd wished to get close to Him so He could bless their children. Jesus' disciples tried to stop them. Perhaps they felt that Jesus was too busy with things more important than blessing children. However, Jesus was displeased with His disciples' attitude and said to them, "Let the children come to Me, and do not hinder them; for to such belongs the kingdom of heaven" (Matt. 19:14, RSV). (*Hold the folded paper firmly and begin to cut out the two figures drawn on it.*)

On another occasion Jesus' disciples asked Him "Who is the greatest in the kingdom of heaven?" (Matt. 18:1). Jesus called a child to Him, set him in the midst of the people, and said to them, "Truly, I say to you, unless you . . . become like children, you shall not enter the kingdom of heaven. Whoever then humbles himself as this child, he is the greatest in the kingdom of heaven" (Matt. 18:3-4, NASB).*

Point out that boys and girls need to know they can be and are expected to be true and faithful disciples of Jesus Christ. Not only through their words, but through their daily actions, they are to give forth a witness for their Master. They can become self-denying, willing daily to take up their cross and follow Him. (*Unfold the cutout figures of the boys and girls and display them to the audience.*)

Challenge them to respond to Christ who waits for their decision, not only to accept Him as Savior, but also to commit themselves to Him as Lord.

Other passages of Scripture you may wish to use are: Matthew 10:32-39; 16:14-16; Luke 14:26-27, 33; John 21: 15-19; Romans 1:16; 5:6-8; 10:3-9; 1 Corinthians 1:4-9, 21-25; 2:1-5; 3:10-17; 2 Corinthians 5:18-19; Galatians 4: 4-5; Ephesians 2:4-10; 1 John 3:5-8; and 4:10.

NOTE: Throughout the latter part of your message, you may wish to present in depth the plan of salvation and the requirements of discipleship. How much material you cover should depend on your audience, the time allotted for your message, and the major emphasis.

*New American Standard Bible.

13

Christ Our Pilot

(*Psalms* 32:8; 73:24)

Materials Needed:

One 18-inch-square sheet of white paper or newspaper
One pair of scissors
One pencil

Instructions for Paper Fold and Cut:

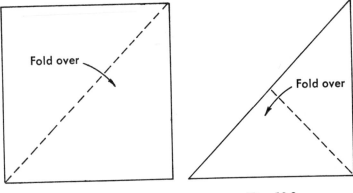

Fig. 13.1   Fig. 13.2

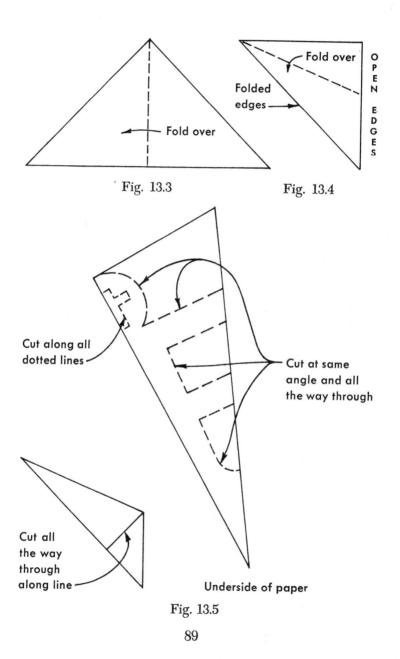

Fold over

Fold over

Folded edges →

O P E N E D G E S

Fig. 13.3   Fig. 13.4

Cut along all dotted lines —

Cut at same angle and all the way through

Cut all the way through along line →

Underside of paper

Fig. 13.5

Fig. 13.6

First, fold the sheet of paper in half diagonally as in figures 13.1 and 13.2.

Second, fold the sheet of paper into quarters diagonally as in figures 13.2 and 13.3.

Third, fold the sheet of paper again diagonally as in figures 13.3 and 13.4.

Fourth, fold the paper diagonally as in figures 13.4 and 13.5. Be sure that all folds are squared off evenly at the edges.

Fifth, on the folded edge of the paper, draw with a pencil the outline of the portion of the pilot's wheel to be cut out as in figure 13.5.

Sixth, at the proper moment in the message, cut along the penciled outline (see fig. 13.5). When cutting the outline, be sure to cut all the way through the outer edges of the upper and inner circles of the pilot's wheel. Also, make sure you cut the bottom line at the angle shown in figure 13.5. If the outline is not cut as shown, the wheel will be in sections instead of a complete circle.

Seventh, at the proper time, unfold the paper and show the completed pilot's wheel to the audience. If it has been folded and cut as explained, it will appear as shown in figure 13.6.

SUGGESTIONS: Prior to demonstrating before your audience, pre-fold the paper and lightly pencil in the outline of the portion of the pilot's wheel to be cut out. Then open the paper so that it appears, from the audience's point of view, that you are folding the paper "from scratch." In the pre-folding, *do not* press the folds. Be sure to make the folds so that they do not have a pre-pressed impression, and that the outline of the pilot's wheel is drawn very lightly so that it can not be seen by the audience.

You will also find that this pilot's wheel, as well as most

of your paper-cutting effects, will be seen best by your audience if you hold it in front of a dark background such as a chalkboard (black or dark green) or a piece of black velvet.

Message:

Your message should center on the theme of Christ as the Pilot of our lives. Once we have accepted Jesus Christ as our personal Savior and Lord, we must give Him control of our lives so that He can guide us in accordance with His will for us.

Go into as much detail as you wish about the duties and need for a pilot when a ship is gliding into a harbor or cruising through unfamiliar waters. The pilot is the guide who gives the instructions as to the course to take and the places to avoid. And as we sail on life's unfamiliar seas, only Christ, our Pilot and Guide, knows the course we should take.

On the sea of life, we will encounter many dangerous areas, and without a proper pilot to guide us, we could easily be shipwrecked. Thus it is very important that we allow Christ to be our Pilot. Go on to talk about the need for a pilot's wheel on every type of ship. The pilot's wheel is needed to guide small and great ships on their courses and brings them safely to their final destination. (*Here you will fold and cut out the pilot's wheel. Open it and show it to your audience.*)

Explain how once we have entrusted our lives to Christ, we need not fear to sail life's sea. He, as our Pilot, will guide us safely to our destination. The appeal of the message should be evangelistic. Point out that everyone of us is aimlessly adrift on the sea of life until we let Christ take over the helm of our life. Through the presence of the

Holy Spirit, Christ is able to teach us the true way, guide our hearts in the right direction and our feet in the way of peace, and lead us with His counsel.

Other Scripture references you may use are: Psalm 27: 11; 31:3; 61:2; 139:9-10, 24; Proverbs 3:5-6; Isaiah 58:11; Luke 1:79; John 16:13; Acts 8:26-40; and Revelation 7:17.

NOTE: If you wish, this message could be combined with the paper-cutting effect shown in chapter eleven, "Anchored in the Safe Harbor of Christ."

14

The Good News for All Mankind

(Matt. 16:24; 28:16-20)

Materials Needed:

    One 8″×11″ sheet of paper in each of the following colors: black, white, red, and yellow

    A pair of scissors

    A pencil

    A black felt pen or large black press-on lettering

Instructions for Paper Fold and Cut:

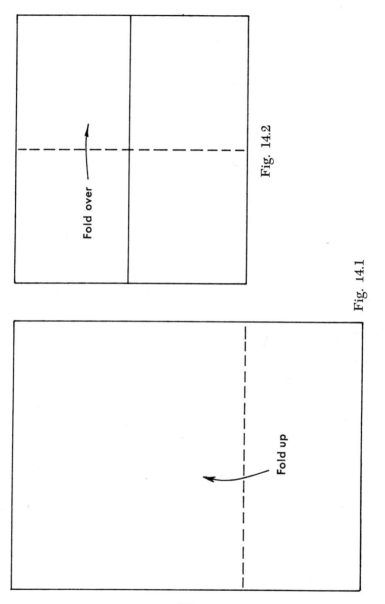

Fold over

Fig. 14.2

Fig. 14.1

Fold up

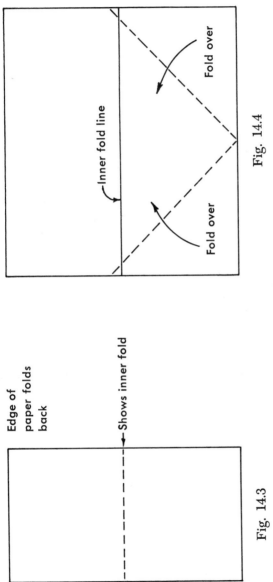

Edge of paper folds back

Shows inner fold

Fig. 14.3

Inner fold line

Fold over

Fold over

Fig. 14.4

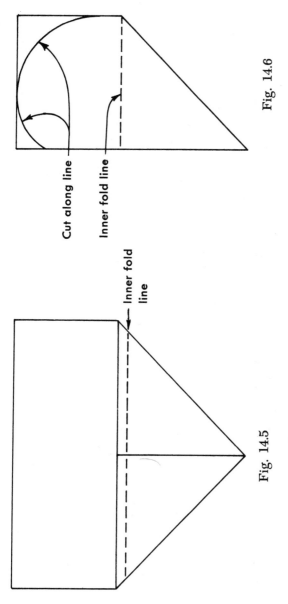

Cut along line

Inner fold line

Fig. 14.6

Inner fold line

Fig. 14.5

97

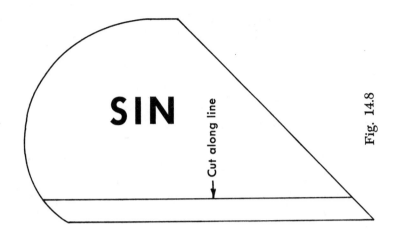

Fig. 14.7

7/16"

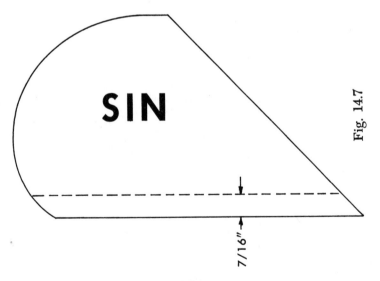

Cut along line

Fig. 14.8

98

Fig. 14.9

First, put all four sheets of paper together evenly, so that they appear as one sheet (see fig. 14.1). Place the white piece of paper on the bottom of the packet so that it faces the audience.

Second, fold up the bottom third of each of the four pieces of paper as in figures 14.1 and 14.2.

Third, then fold the four pieces of paper in half from left to right as in figures 14.2 and 14.3; then unfold them.

Fourth, fold the left and right bottom corners of the sheets at right angles toward the center of the paper as in figures 14.4 and 14.5.

Fifth, now refold the sheets of paper in half, as in figure 14.6 and draw lightly with a pencil the outline of the top half of a heart (see fig. 14.6).

Sixth, then draw lightly with a pencil a line seven-sixteenth of an inch from the folded edge of the white sheet of paper and print with a black felt pen, or large press-on lettering, the word SIN as in figure 14.7.

Seventh, at the proper moment in the message, cut along the line at the top of the pieces of paper (see fig. 14.6) and open them out to form a heart. The white sheet should be facing the audience. Keeping the bottom folds in place, take the four pieces of paper apart, showing the audience a white, a black, a red, and a yellow heart.

Eighth, at the right time, put the four hearts, with the white one on top, back together as before. Refold the pieces of paper (see fig. 14.8) and cut along the straight line to cut off the word SIN (see fig. 14.8). Then unfold the pieces of paper displaying to the audience a cross. Take them apart and show the audience a white, a black, a red, and a yellow cross (see fig. 14.9).

SUGGESTION: You will find it helpful to lightly fold

the white sheet of paper ahead of time and print the word *SIN* in the correct position.

Message:

I usually start this message by making reference to man's natural inclination to sin because he is born with a sinful nature (Gen. 3; Rom. 5:12-19; 1 Cor. 15:22). I also emphasize that man's heart is desperately wicked and in need of cleansing (Jer. 17:9-10; Rom. 6:23; 1 John 1:7b-10).

(*At this point, fold the four sheets of paper, cut out the* hearts and show them *unseparated to the audience [see figs. 14.1-14.7]. Be sure to keep the white heart with the* "SIN," *which you printed ahead of time, in front.*)

Explain the importance of having our hearts cleansed from sin through faith in the atoning work of Jesus Christ on Calvary. Explain God's plan of salvation in easily understood terms. Start with the importance of acknowledging the fact that all mankind have sinned and fallen far short of the glory of God (Rom. 3:23; Gal. 3:22; 1 John 1:10). (*Emphasize the word* ALL *by taking apart the four sheets of paper and showing the audience that you now have four hearts—white, black, red, and yellow.*)

Explain that Christ came not to save just one select group of people, but that He gave His life as a ransom for all mankind. This includes the black people of Africa and other parts of the world; the yellow people of China, Japan, Korea, and elsewhere; the red-skinned Indians—the native Americans and others; plus the white people of America, Europe, South and Central America and other places.

Second, point out that it is impossible for any people to save themselves for salvation is by God's grace and not by human efforts (Rom. 11:6, 32; Eph. 2:8-9). Also emphasize that they must hear the good news if they are to be saved. Thus our responsibility of sharing the gospel with them is one of our privileges as disciples (Matt. 28:18-20; Rom. 10:14-15).

Third, stress that God loved the entire world so much that He was willing to give His only Son to die that all mankind might be reconciled to Him through faith (John 3:16; 5:24). Therefore, we who claim to follow Christ as Lord must start in our own neighborhoods and then move out to the uttermost parts of the earth to proclaim the good news of salvation through faith in Christ's atoning work (Matt. 28:18-20; Mark 16:14-15).

You may wish to refer to some of the following passages of Scripture: Matthew 1:21; 18:11; Luke 18:19; John 5: 24; 16:7-11; Acts 2:21; 4:12; 15:11; Romans 5:8; 10:8-13; 1 Corinthians 15:3; 2 Corinthians 6:2; Titus 3:1-8; and 1 Peter 3:18.

(*After you have talked about the need to be forgiven of sin in order to be reconciled with God, refold the four sheets of paper and cut off the word* SIN *[see fig. 14.8]. As you reopen the folded sheets of paper, show the audience the four crosses [see fig. 14.9] as you quote Matt. 16:24.*)

Now stress your second major point, that a faithful disciple bears his cross and follows Christ. Emphasize that as we witness for Christ, whether at home or on the foreign field, we will be called upon to make sacrifices for the cause of our Master. Tell how *all* who claim Christ as their personal Savior have this responsibility and privilege. Therefore, it is not the obligation of an elite group of people. All of us, whether black, red, yellow, or white, as followers of Christ are to be His ambassadors. We are called to represent Him as pastors, or teachers, or missionaries, or witnesses in a secular job—whatever our life-style or occupation, we each have the privilege of taking up our cross and following Christ wherever He leads.

You may wish to refer to these passages of Scripture for additional insight into this aspect of truth: Acts 4:18-20; 5:29-32; Romans 12:1-6; Galatians 2:20; Ephesians 4:7; and Philipians 3:4-14.

NOTE: If you desire, conclude your message by either quoting or singing one of the following hymns: "We've a Story to Tell to the Nations"; "O Zion, Haste"; "You Servants of God, Your Master Proclaim"; "Must Jesus Bear the Cross Alone?"; "Jesus Calls Us"; or "I'll Go Where You Want Me to Go."

15

Faithfulness in Discipleship

(*Matt. 25:21; Rev. 2:10*)

Materials Needed:

One 10″×14″ sheet of paper
One pair of scissors
One black felt pen or press-on lettering
One pencil

Instructions for Paper Fold and Cut:

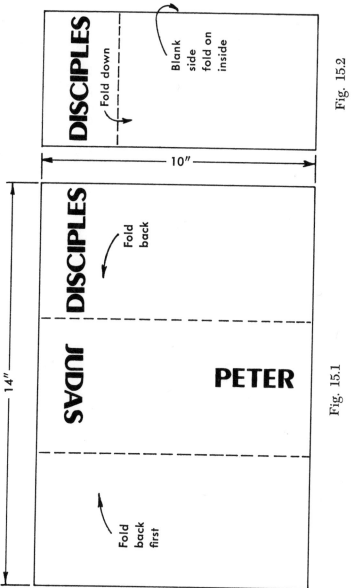

Fig. 15.2

Fold down

Blank side fold on inside

DISCIPLES

DISCIPLES

Fold back

JUDAS

PETER

Fold back first

Fig. 15.1

10"

14"

105

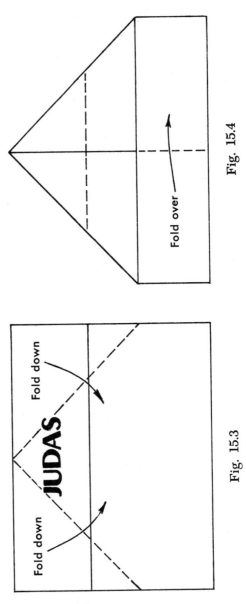

Fig. 15.4

Fig. 15.3

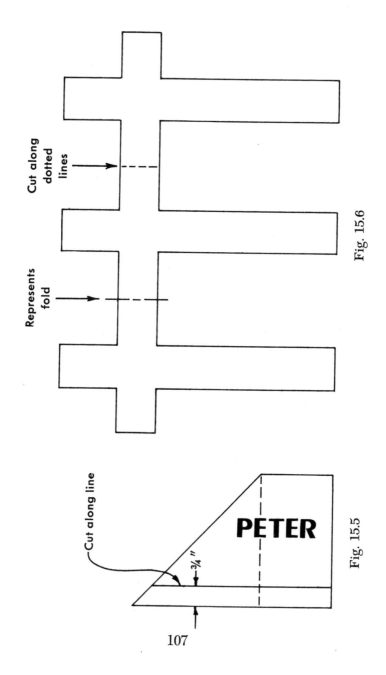

Cut along dotted lines

Represents fold

Fig. 15.6

Cut along line

3/4 "

PETER

107

Fig. 15.5

First, fold the sheet of paper into thirds following this sequence (see fig. 15.1): Fold the blank third of the sheet to your left behind the center section. Then fold the third of the sheet with the word *DISCIPLES* printed on it behind the center section over the blank folded third of the sheet.

Second, unfold the paper and print the words on it *exactly* as shown in figure 15.1. Be sure to make the lettering large enough to be easily read by your audience.

Third, at the proper moment in the message, fold the sheet of paper into thirds as explained in step one. Then, after talking about the disciples, fold the top portion of the sheet down (see fig. 15.2), displaying the word *JUDAS* (see fig. 15.3).

Fourth, after talking about Judas, fold the left and right upper corners of the sheet of paper at right angles toward the center of the sheet. This will then cover the word *JUDAS* (see figs. 15.3 and 15.4).

Fifth, fold the sheet of paper in half, displaying the word *PETER* as in figures 15.4 and 15.5.

Sixth, at the right moment in the message, cut along the line shown in figure 15.5. Unfold the cut portion of the paper and display three crosses joined together as in figure 15.6.

Seventh, when you are talking about the two thieves who died on the crosses on either side of Christ, cut along the dotted lines (see fig. 15.6) and discard the single cross. Show the audience the two crosses still joined together, representing the penitent thief who found fellowship with Christ through faith.

Message:

Ahead of time, fold the sheet of paper into thirds and

do the lettering as in figure 15.1.

The introduction to your message should emphasize our need to be faithful disciples of Christ, once we have accepted Him as our personal Savior and Lord. Quote Revelation 2:10. You may wish to refer to the parable of the talents told by Jesus, in Matthew 25:14-30, or to Jesus' dialogue with reluctant followers, recorded in Luke 9:57-62.

After the introduction, relate the events of the closing days of Christ's life, as recorded in Luke 22:39–23:46 and Matthew 26:17-75. Beginning with the Last Supper in the upper room, tell how Jesus warned His disciples that they would be tested because of Him. Mention Peter's bold declaration of faithfulness to the Master (Matt. 26:33).

Move the scene from the upper room to the Garden of Gethsemane. Tell how Christ asked all of His disciples, but especially Peter, James, and John, to watch and pray with Him. Instead, He found them sleeping. They were more concerned with their own needs than those of their Leader. Because of their indifference and unfaithfulness, when the real hour of testing came, they all forsook Him and ran away (Matt. 26:56b). (*Show the sheet of paper folded as in fig. 15.2. Fold down the upper portion demonstrating how the disciples broke their fellowship with Christ and failed to be faithful disciples.*)

(*This also shows the name of Judas [fig. 15.3].*) Tell how he was a disciple of Jesus, yet for a mere thirty pieces of silver, he led the angry "crowd with swords and clubs, from the chief priests and the elders of the people" (Matt. 26:47, RSV) to the Garden of Gethsemane where he betrayed Christ with a kiss. So Judas, a professing follower and disciple broke his fellowship with Jesus by betraying Him. (*Fold the two upper corners of the sheet of paper [see figs. 15.3 and 15.4] to show how Judas failed his test of faithfulness.*)

(*Next, fold the sheet of paper in half, as in fig. 15.5, displaying the name* Peter.) Relate the account of Christ's illegal trials and how Peter, after first running away, decided to follow Jesus to the courtyard of the high priest, Caiaphas (Matt. 26:58). There he who had boasted so loudly and confidently that he would die rather than betray his Master, when faced with the possibility of arrest, turned coward and denied his Lord three times (Matt. 26:69-75). If we, who are Christ's disciples, do not stand up for Him when the going is difficult, our fellowship with Him will be cut off. (*Now cut along the penciled line [see fig. 15.5]. Leave the long narrow strip of paper still folded.*)

Although we may not be faithful disciples, He still loves us and longs for us to be reconciled to Him. He is ever willing to forgive us and restore us to fellowship as He did with Peter and the other ten disciples.

Lead from this phase of the message into the crucifixion scene. Tell how Christ was crucified between two thieves. Get your details from Matthew 27:32-50 and Luke 23:26-49. (*Open out the folded strip of paper and reveal the three crosses linked together [see fig. 15.6]*). Relate that at first the attitude of both criminals, on either side of Christ's cross, was the same. Then one of them had a change of heart. He acknowledged Christ as his Master and asked Him to remember him when He came into His kingdom (Luke 23:40-43). At that exact moment, he was forgiven and united in fellowship with Christ. The other thief did not repent and acknowledge Christ as Lord; thus he died outside the fellowship of Jesus. (*Cut along the dotted lines [see fig. 15.6] and show how two of the crosses*

110

are united, but the other one is separated from the cross of Christ.)

Conclude by mentioning our need to be cross-bearers if we would be faithful disciples and continue to have unbroken fellowship with Christ.

Other relevant passages of Scripture are: Matthew 10:38; 16:24; Mark 8:34; 10:21; Luke 14:27; 16:10-13; John 8:31; 13:35; 15:8; 1 Corinthians 4:2; Galatians 6:12, 14; Ephesians 2:16; 3:14-19; Philippians 1:5-6; 2:8; 2 Timothy 2:2-3; James 1:12; 1 Peter 5:1-4; and 1 John 1:3, 6-7.

16

A Believer's Two Natures

(Rom. 7:13-25; Eph. 4:17-32; Col. 3:5-10)

Materials Needed:

Four 8½"×11" sheets of white construction paper, one
  heavily blotched with black felt pen
One 8½"×11" sheet of red construction paper
One sheet of legal size typewriter paper
One pencil
One fine-point black felt pen
One regular black felt pen
One ruler
One tube of glue or paste
One pair of sharp scissors

Instructions for Paper Fold and Cut:

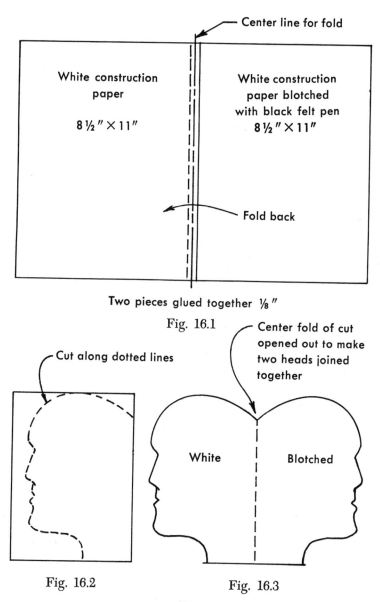

Center line for fold

White construction paper

8½" × 11"

White construction paper blotched with black felt pen

8½" × 11"

Fold back

Two pieces glued together ⅛"

Fig. 16.1

Cut along dotted lines

Center fold of cut opened out to make two heads joined together

White

Blotched

Fig. 16.2

Fig. 16.3

STEP I:

First, use a black felt pen to make blotches on one of the white sheets of art paper. Glue together the white and the blotched sheets, allowing a one-eighth-inch overlap (see fig. 16.1).

Second, fold the glued pieces of paper in half, with the blotched piece behind the white piece (see figs. 16.1 and 16.2).

Third, with a pencil sketch very lightly the pattern of a face profile on the top white sheet of paper (see fig. 16.2).

Fourth, at the proper time in the message, cut along the dotted lines, thus forming a single face profile.

Fifth, unfold the piece of paper showing two face profiles joined together—one white and the other blotched (see fig. 16.3). These will represent a believer's old nature (disfigured by sin) and his new nature in Christ (cleansed by His blood).

STEP II:

First, glue together two sheets of stiff white paper as in figure 16.4.

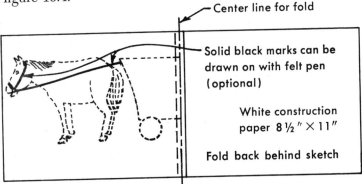

Center line for fold

Solid black marks can be drawn on with felt pen (optional)

White construction paper 8 ½ " × 11"

Fold back behind sketch

Two pieces glued together ⅛ "

Fig. 16.4

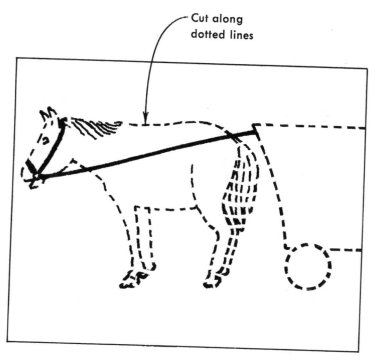

Cut along dotted lines

Fig. 16.5

Fig. 16.6

Second, fold in half the glued paper. Fold the right side behind the left side as in figure 16.4.

Third, lightly pencil in the pattern of a horse and part of a wagon on the top piece of paper, as in figures 16.4 and 16.5.

Fourth, at the proper moment in the message, cut out the pattern, unfold the paper, and show the two horses, with the cart between them, pulling against each other to represent the struggle that goes on within us between the old and new natures.

Fifth, this is optional. If you are artistic, you may fill in details, such as, reins, eyes, horse bridle, and so forth.

STEP III:

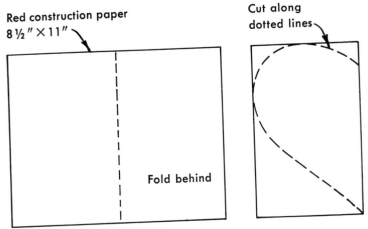

Red construction paper
8 ½ " × 11 "

Fold behind

Fig. 16.7

Cut along
dotted lines

Fig. 16.8

Fig. 16.9

First, fold in half an 8½″× 11″ sheet of red construction paper. Fold the right side behind the left side as in figures 16.7 and 16.8.

Second, sketch on the front half of the folded sheet the pattern of a half heart (see fig. 16.8).

Third, at the right moment in your message, cut out the pattern, unfold the piece of construction paper, and show a large red heart to your audience (see fig. 16.9).

STEP IV:

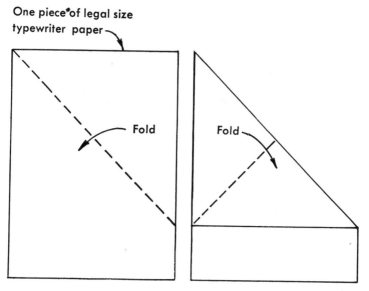

One piece of legal size typewriter paper

Fold

Fold

Fig. 16.10

Fig. 16.11

117

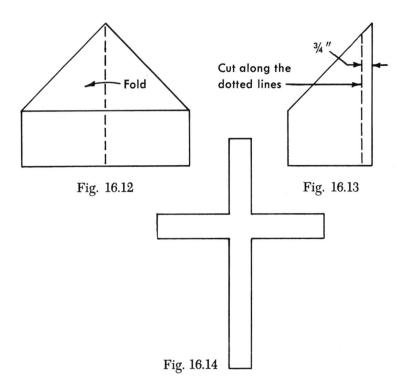

Fig. 16.12

¾ "

Cut along the dotted lines →

Fig. 16.13

Fig. 16.14

First, take a piece of legal size typewriter paper and fold the right upper corner down to form a right angle with the left edge of the paper (see fig. 16.10).

Second, fold the left upper corner of the paper down toward the right edge of the paper forming a 45° triangle (see fig. 16.11).

Third, fold the piece of paper in half, right to left (see fig. 16.12). Pencil a straight line ¾ inch from the folded edge (see fig. 16.13).

Fourth, at the proper moment in your message, cut along the dotted lines (fig. 16.13), and when you unfold the paper it will form a cross as in figure 16.14.

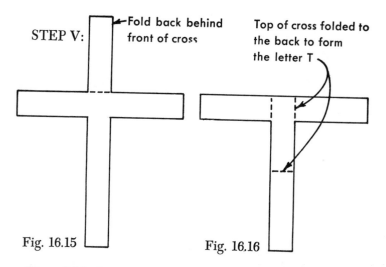

STEP V:

←Fold back behind front of cross

Top of cross folded to the back to form the letter T

Fig. 16.15

Fig. 16.16

First, fold the top of the cross to the back as in figure 16.15. Make sure the fold is neat so that it forms a straight line across the arm of the cross.

Second, show the audience that the cross has now been formed into the letter *T* which will represent the word *truth* (see fig. 16.16).

STEP VI:

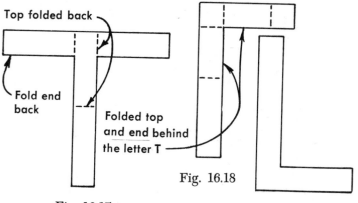

Top folded back

Fold end back

Folded top and end behind the letter T

Fig. 16.17

Fig. 16.18

Fig. 16.19

119

First, fold the left corner of the letter *T* to the back (see fig. 16.17).

Second, turn the piece of paper, as in figure 16.18, upside down to form the letter *L*. With the index finger and thumb of your left hand, hold firmly the top and end of the cross, which are folded to the back. When shown to the audience, the letter *T* will now form the letter *L* representing *LIFE* (see fig. 16.19).

STEP VII:

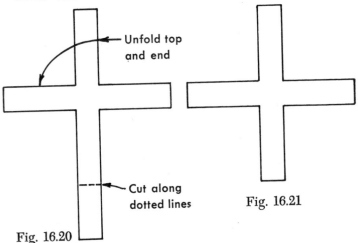

← Unfold top and end

← Cut along dotted lines

Fig. 16.21

Fig. 16.20

First, unfold the top and end that were turned back to form the letter *L*, thus forming the cross as it was in STEP V (see fig. 16.15).

Second, make sure that the dotted lines are marked so as to make a perfect "plus" sign as in figure 16.21.

Third, cut off the bottom portion of the cross along the dotted lines (see fig. 16.20). Show this sign to your audience to represent the "plus" that comes into the life of a Christian when he fully yields to Christ and allows his new nature to bear the fruit of the Spirit.

Message:

One important truth taught in the Word of God is that even though we have accepted Jesus Christ as our Savior, we still have a struggle going on within us. This is the battle between the old sinful nature we inherited from Adam and our new righteous nature we received from Christ. Perhaps you, like so many recent believers in Christ, thought that once you had put your trust in Him, all your problems would be solved, especially your battles with temptation. However, you soon found out that this was not so. You still desired to do some things you knew were wrong. In fact, it seemed as though the devil was really out to get you and was determined to make you yield to his temptations.

You might have given up your new faith in despair if you had not learned that you now had a power within you to assist you in fighting Satan's temptations. When you became a Christian, you received a new nature that made it possible for you to live a Christlike life and win the struggle with your old sinful nature. (*Following the instructions under STEP I, fold and cut out the profile of the face [see figs. 16.1 and 16.2]. Unfold the paper and show your audience the two profiles [see fig. 16.3].*)

The old sinful nature, which we inherited from Adam, is not removed when we are born again, and it is the cause of much of our failure to become spiritually mature (see Gen. 3; Rom. 5:12). John, in his first epistle, admits to the fact of indwelling sin in believers' lives when he writes, "If we say that we have no sin, we deceive ourselves, and the truth is not in us" (1 John 1:8). Paul, in his letter to the church in Rome, refers to his personal problem of inner struggle between his old and new natures. He says that they are constantly wrestling with each other, and, unless at the very beginning of the conflict, his new nature gets the upper hand, he is in trouble (Rom. 7:15-25).

Discuss the importance of feeding the new nature through Bible study, prayer, church attendance, and faithful service. If we do not feed the new nature, it becomes weak, the old nature takes over, and we fall away from Christ and His will for our lives (Rom. 7:16-20; Gal. 5:17-21). (*To demonstrate the struggle between our two natures, cut out the pattern of the horse and cart, which you have drawn ahead of time, following the instructions in STEP II [see figs. 16.4 and 16.5]. Unfold the sheet of paper and show the two horses struggling against each other to pull the cart [see fig. 16.6].*)

Give illustrations of how some disciples have struggled and learned the secret of living victoriously in Christ. You can use Paul's personal testimony or relate your own growth experience to your present commitment to Christ.

Emphasize that many Christians live defeated, frustrated lives because they give in to their old natures. They have not grown spiritually strong enough to win the battle over self and sin. They are miserable because they are producing the fruit of their old nature, which is the lust of the flesh (Gal. 5:17-21).

However, it is Christ's will that we who have trusted Him as Savior and Lord should live victorious lives. This is possible when we open up our lives to the Holy Spirit's control (emphasize Rom. 8:1-2). Then He frees us from the "law of sin and death" and gives us power to win over the old nature. When we yield ourselves to the Holy Spirit, we become vibrant, happy, victorious Christians who daily produce in our lives the fruit of the Spirit: "love, joy, peace, patience, kindness, goodness, faithfulness, gentleness, self-control" (Gal. 5:22-23, RSV).

Mention that, if our new nature is to grow, we must let Christ, who indwells us through His Holy Spirit (Eph. 3: 16-17), have complete control of our hearts. (*Following the instructions under STEP III, fold and cut out the pattern of the heart [see figs. 16.7 and 16.8]. Show the half of a heart to the audience first.*) Talk about the many Christians who constantly live defeated lives. These individuals are halfhearted Christians. They are holding back from a complete commitment to the Holy Spirit's control of their lives. What they and we need is to become wholehearted Christians. (*Unfold the heart and show it to the audience.*)

Talk about the importance of being fully-committed followers of Christ. Only as we allow His will to be done in our lives can we be victorious over the old nature.

Use such Scriptures as Ephesians 3:16-19; 5:19-20; 6:6*b*-8; Philippians 4:6-8; Colossians 3:12-17; 2 Thessalonians 3:3-5; Hebrews 10:22-23; James 4:8; and 1 Peter 3:15 as the basis for this part of your message. You may also use as illustrations individuals who became wholehearted followers of Christ and whose lives have been a means of blessing to others.

This should lead you into the next point: namely, this abundant life is made available to us through faith in Jesus Christ, who gave Himself as a ransom for us. He paid the debt for our sin on the cross that we might be set free from that debt and live victorious over sin's control (Matt. 20:28; 1 Timothy 2:3-6). (*Following the instructions given in STEP IV, fold and cut out the pattern of the cross [see figs. 16.10-16.14]. Unfold the cross and show it to the audience.*)

Continue your message by saying that because Christ willingly died that we might be reconciled to God the

Father, we have the privilege of denying ourselves, taking up our cross, and faithfully following Him (Mark 8:34). This means that Christ must become our Lord as well as our Savior. Then, we become crucified to worldly things (Gal. 6:14) and are transformed into the image of Jesus Christ (Rom. 8:29). We are not only justified and glorified but also are secure in Him through faith (Rom. 8:28-39).

Other passages of Scripture you may wish to refer to while speaking on the cross are: Philippians 2:5-8; Colossians 1:19-21; Hebrews 12:2.

(*At this point take the cross [see fig. 16.14] and following the instructions under STEP V, fold back the top of the cross to form the letter* T *[see figs. 16.15 and 16.16].* As you hold the letter *T*, talk of the importance of knowing, believing, and acting upon the *truth* of the Word of God, if we would be victorious Christians.

Numerous passages from the Bible can be used to develop this portion of your message. A few that I have used are: John 8:32; 14:6; 16:13; 17:17; 2 Timothy 2:15; 3:1-17; 1 John 3:18-19; 5:6; Ephesians 4:17-32; and 1 Corinthians 13. Emphasize the importance of believing in the inspiration of the Scriptures, the Word of God, and allowing the Holy Spirit to apply their truths to our lives, if we are to win the struggle between our old and new natures. We must accept, believe, and act upon the Scriptures because they are *truth*.

Move on to the subject of *life*. (*Following the instructions under STEP VI, change the letter* T *into the letter* L *[see figs. 16.17-16.19].*)

Show the letter *L* to your audience, stating that it refers to *life*. Here you will want to emphasize not only eternal life, which is ours through faith in Jesus Christ, but also the abundant life that is available to us *now* through our obedience to Christ as He reveals Himself to us through the Word (see John 14:21, 23).

The following references will help you develop this truth: Matthew 7:13-14; John 10:10, 28; 14:6; 17:1-3; Romans 6:1-23 (especially vv. 6 and 8); Galatians 2:20; Ephesians 2:1-10; Colossians 3:1-10; and 1 John 5:12-13.

Conclude by saying that as mature Christians, all of us should be "plus" individuals in our communities, making them better places to live in because we reflect our Lord's standards and life-style. (*Follow the instructions under STEP VII [see figs. 16.20 and 16.21]. Show the audience how you have turned the cross into a plus sign.*) We need to witness to His grace by our lives. We need to be "plus" Christians who bear the fruit of the Spirit daily (Gal. 5:22-24) and prove, by our standards and life-styles, that we have been truly crucified with Christ (Gal. 2:20). Point out that a "plus" Christian is one in whom other people are able to see Christ's characteristics being reproduced by the power of the Holy Spirit.

NOTE 1: I have given this message as an example to show how several paper fold-and-cuts can be combined to present a full length sermon on any essential truth from the Bible. I believe such an example will help you to develop sermons of your own by combining two or more paper folds and cuts into one message.

NOTE 2: This type of message can be easily changed as far as the order is concerned. You might wish to start out with the cross, presenting the plan of salvation and then talking of the Christian's two natures. There are numerous possibilities. Just allow the Holy Spirit to guide your thinking and stimulate your creativity.

One Last Word

It has been a joy putting together these sixteen illustrated messages for children. The impression of "magic" in most of them will increase their impact on those who see them. I pray that you will use these object lessons for the glory of God and the proclamation of the gospel of Jesus Christ. Allow the Holy Spirit to guide you in your preparation and presentation.

Before you present one of these messages to an audience, practice the folds until you feel comfortable doing them and know they are being done correctly. Do the actual cutting so that you can see the finished product. You must feel confident that the particular effect will work and convey the message to your audience. The only way I know to build this kind of confidence is through *practice*. Aim for that point of perfection where you do not have to look at your hands while you are making the folds. Maintain eye contact with your audience. Do not stop to look at your hands or the sheet of paper while you are folding it. Do not settle for anything less than your very best when you are presenting the life-changing truths of the Word of God.

I am sure that, as you have read these messages, you have been motivated to develop messages of your own. I pray that you will be encouraged to do so. Certain of the folds used in chapter 13, "Christ Our Pilot," can be used for cutting a beautiful snowflake or a string of fish. The fold used in chapter 7, "God's Time Is Important," can be used to cut the outline of a church or loaves and fish. The more you work with and use paper folding and cutting, the more creative you will become.

If you have been blessed through the use of any of these messages or some creative ones of your own, I would be happy to hear from you.

Finally, let me urge you to present these, and any other object lessons you might use, in a worshipful manner. May your one desire be to exalt our Lord by winning some lost person to Jesus Christ, who is the Way, the Truth, and the Life.

HAROLD P. WELLS
Chaplain (LTC), USA
Office of the Staff Chaplain
Aberdeen Proving Ground,
Maryland 21005

Moody Press, a ministry of the Moody Bible Institute, is designed for education, evangelization, and edification. If we may assist you in knowing more about Christ and the Christian life, please write us without obligation: Moody Press, c/o MLM, Chicago, Illinois 60610.